DOG BUTTS AND LOVE.
AND STUFF LIKE THAT.
AND CATS.

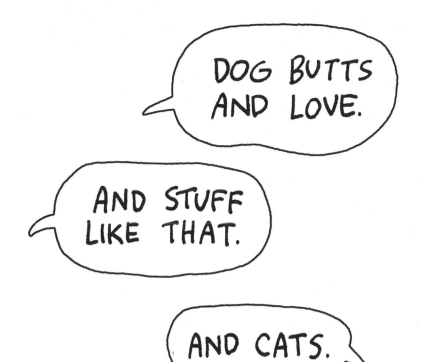

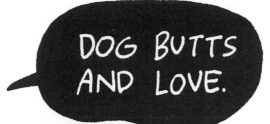

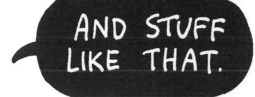

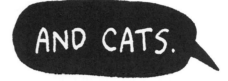

DOG BUTTS AND LOVE. AND STUFF LIKE THAT. AND CATS.

JIM BENTON

DEAD SHIT

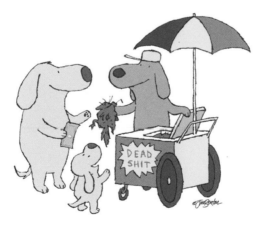

NANTIER • BEALL • MINOUSTCHINE
Publishing inc.
new york

ISBN 9781561638468

Library of Congress Control Number: 2014933513
1st printing July 2014
Printed in China

This is also available wherever e-books are sold

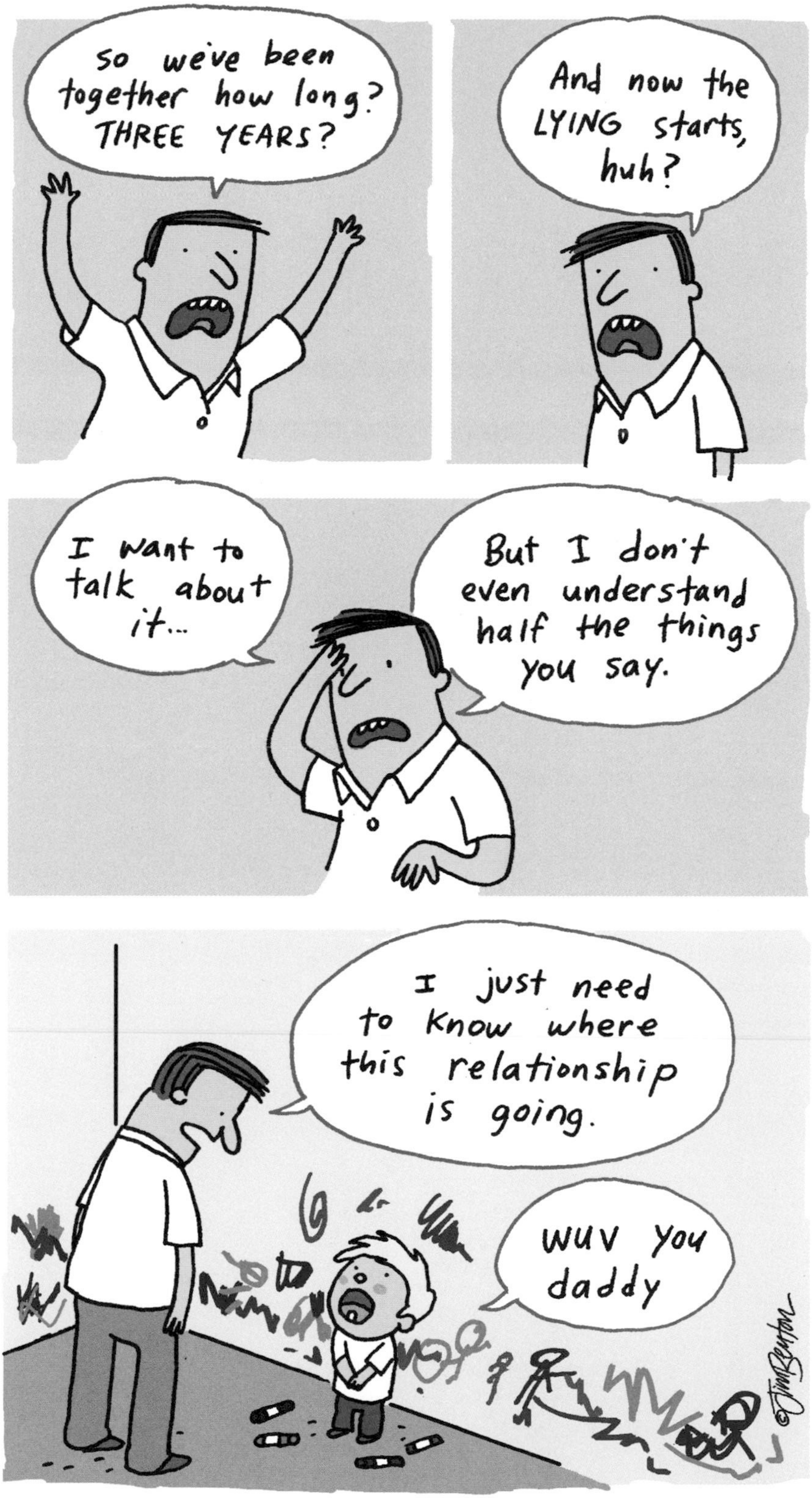
So we've been together how long? THREE YEARS?
And now the LYING starts, huh?
I want to talk about it...
But I don't even understand half the things you say.
I just need to know where this relationship is going.
WUV you daddy
©Jim Benton

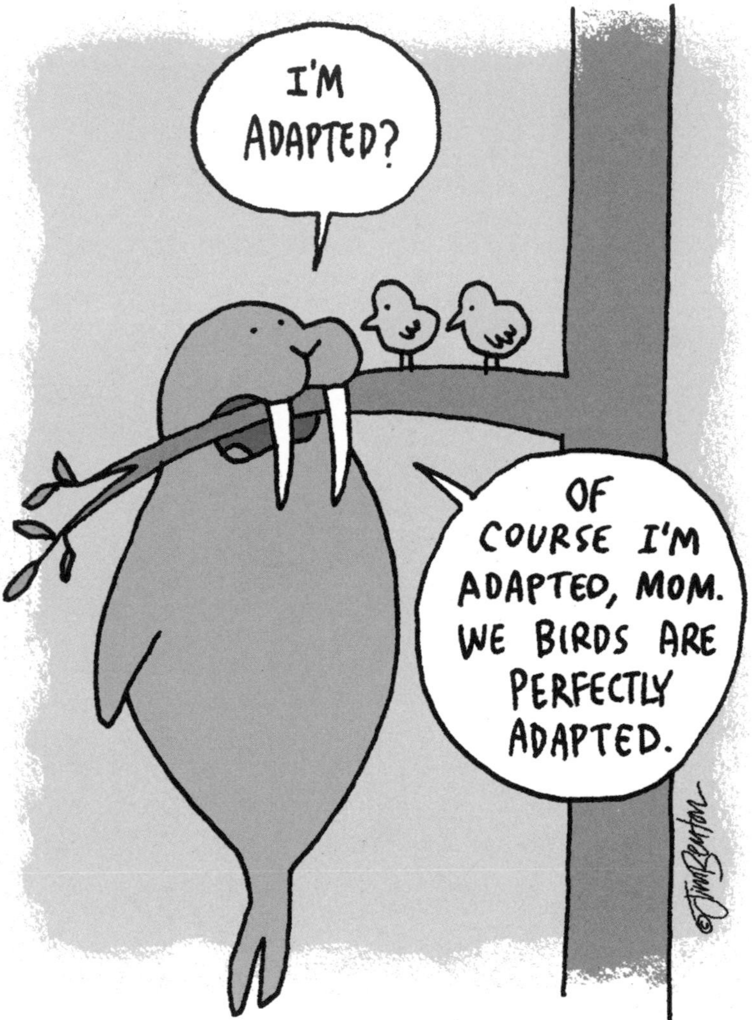
I'M ADAPTED?
OF COURSE I'M ADAPTED, MOM. WE BIRDS ARE PERFECTLY ADAPTED.

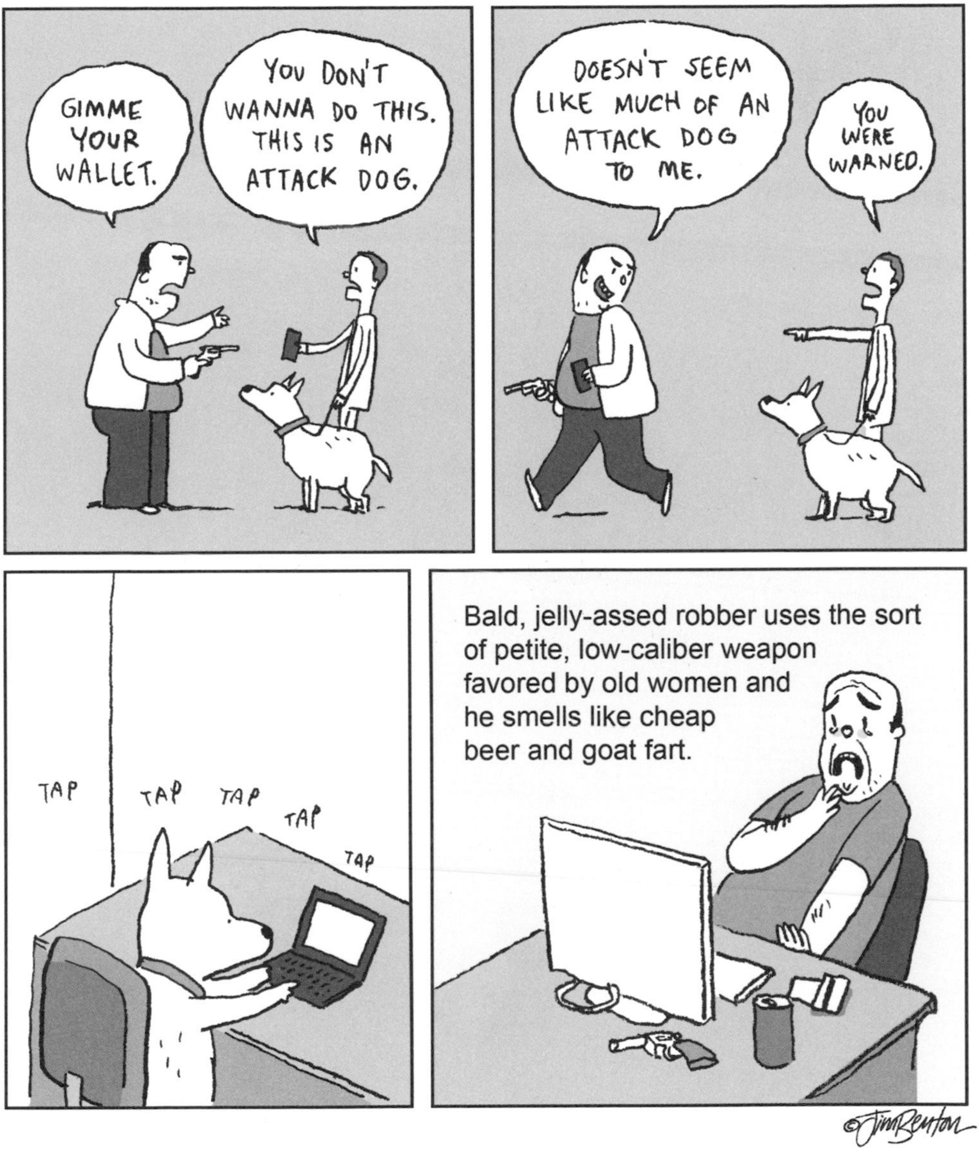
GIMME YOUR WALLET.
YOU DON'T WANNA DO THIS. THIS IS AN ATTACK DOG.
DOESN'T SEEM LIKE MUCH OF AN ATTACK DOG TO ME.
YOU WERE WARNED.
TAP
TAP
TAP
TAP
TAP
Bald, jelly-assed robber uses the sort of petite, low-caliber weapon favored by old women and he smells like cheap beer and goat fart.
©Jim Benton

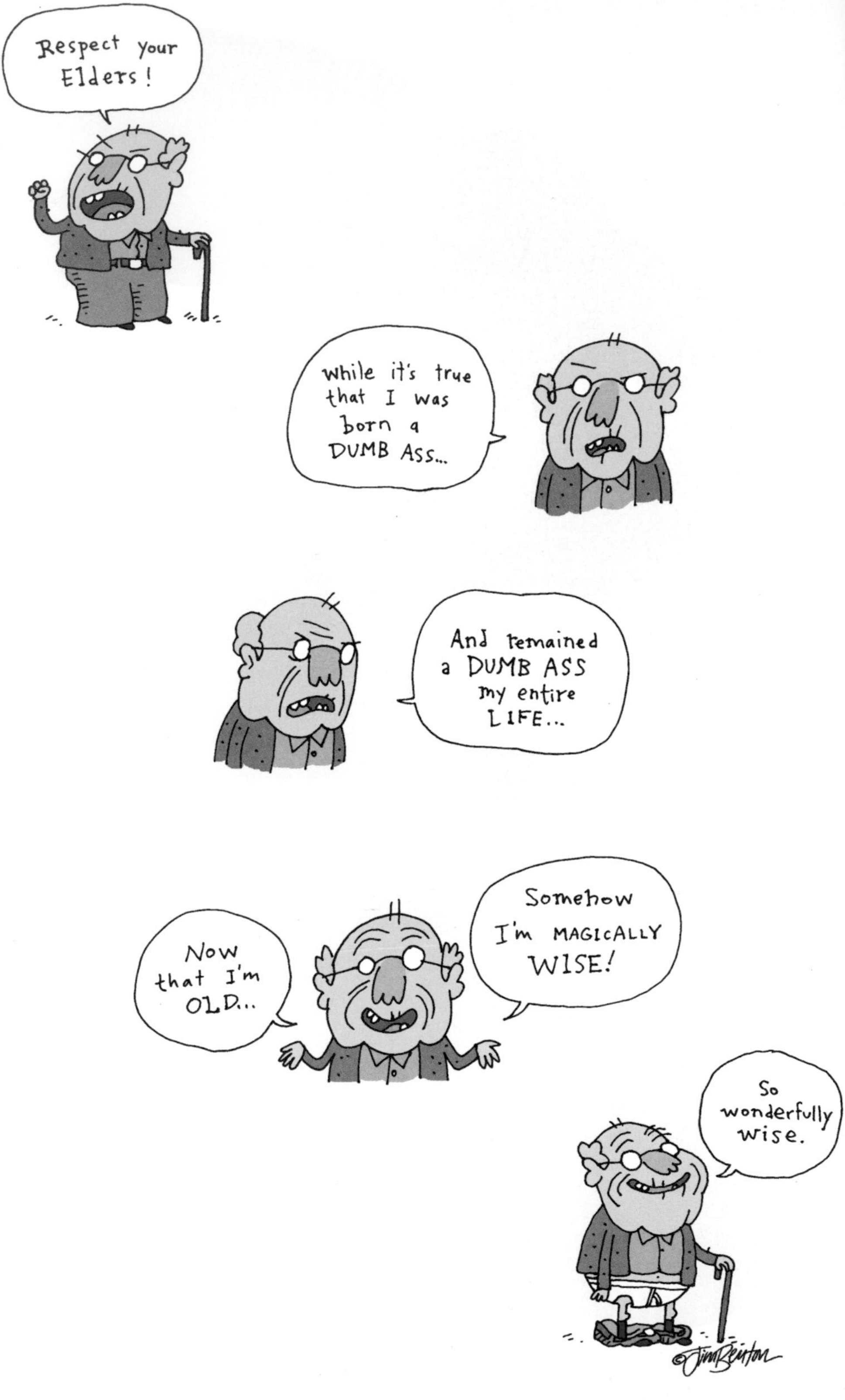
Respect your Elders!
While it's true that I was born a DUMB ASS...
And remained a DUMB ASS my entire LIFE...
Now that I'm OLD...
Somehow I'm MAGICALLY WISE!
So wonderfully wise.
©Jim Benton

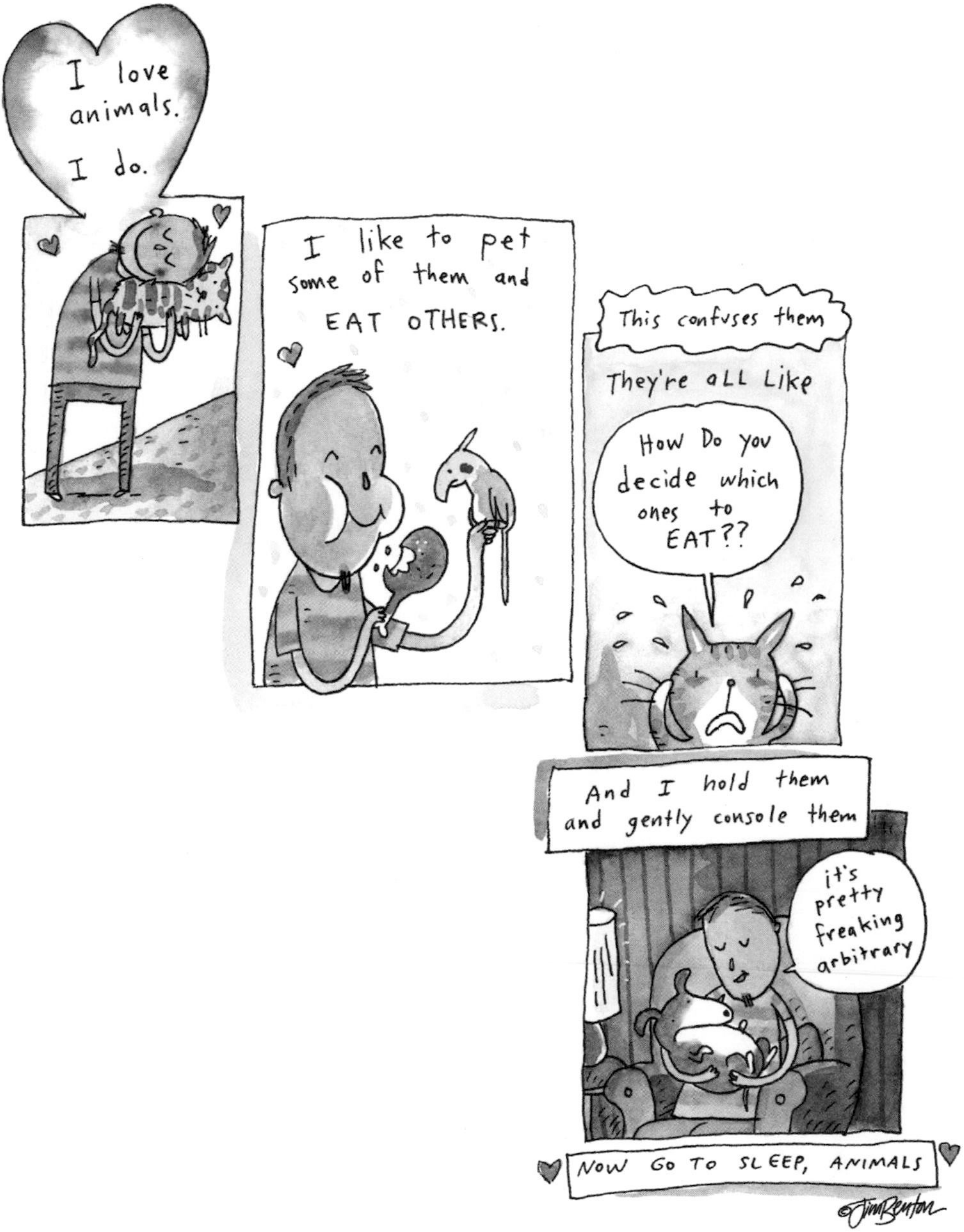
I love animals. I do.
I like to pet some of them and EAT OTHERS.
This confuses them
They're aLL Like
How Do you decide which ones to EAT??
And I hold them and gently console them
it's pretty freaking arbitrary
Now Go To SLEEP, ANIMALS
©Jim Benton

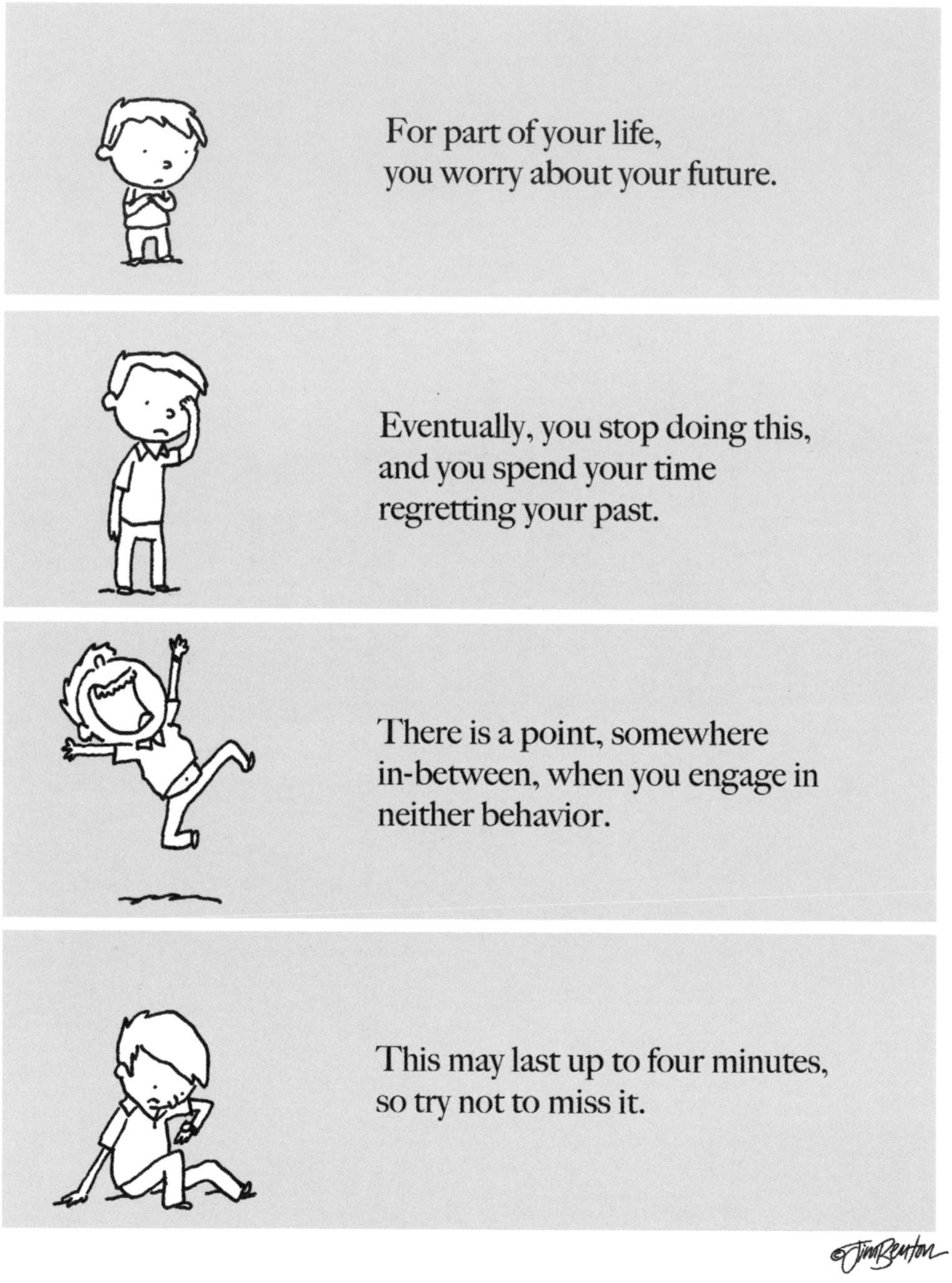
For part of your life, you worry about your future.
Eventually, you stop doing this, and you spend your time regretting your past.
There is a point, somewhere in-between, when you engage in neither behavior.
This may last up to four minutes, so try not to miss it.
©Jim Benton

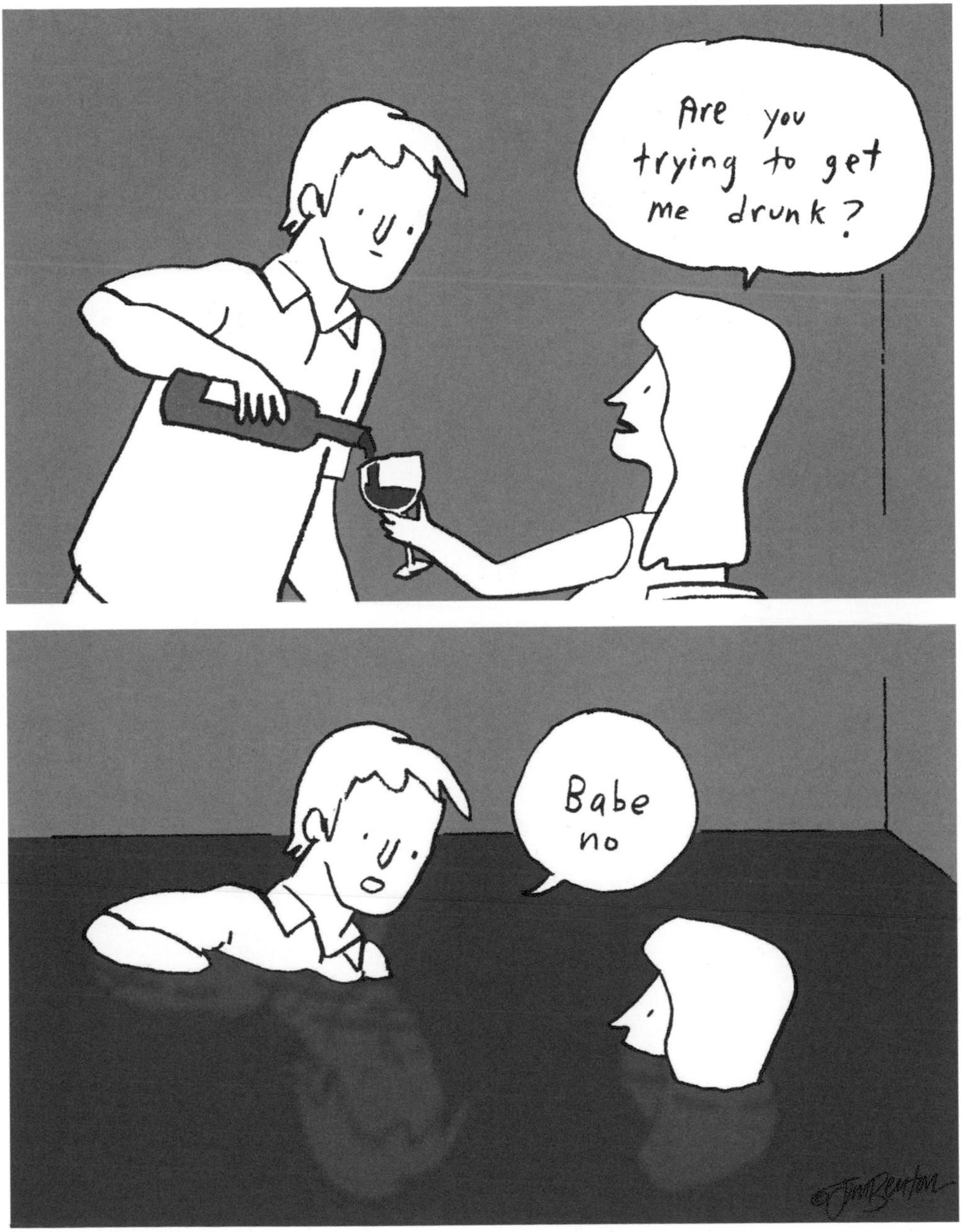
Are you trying to get me drunk?
Babe no

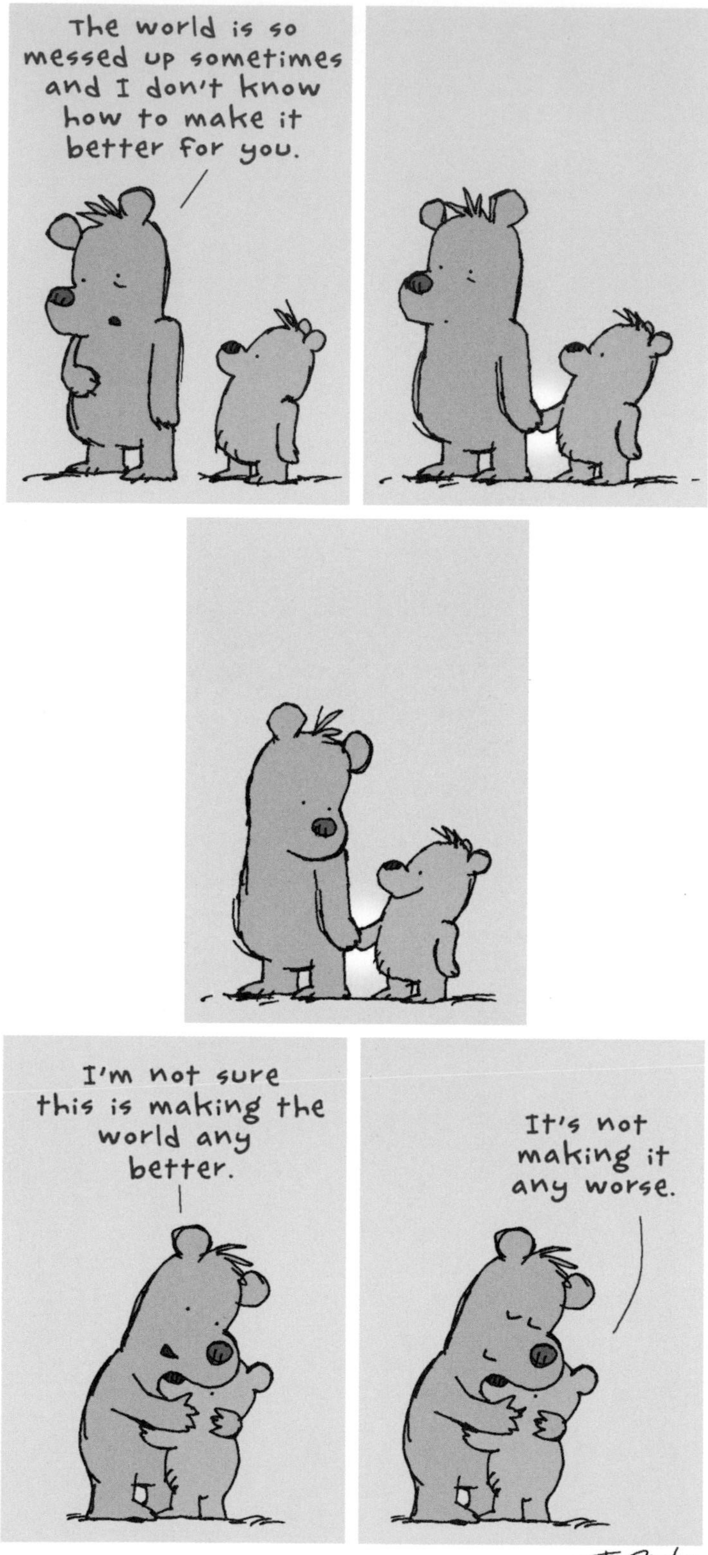
The world is so messed up sometimes and I don't know how to make it better for you.
I'm not sure this is making the world any better.
It's not making it any worse.
©Jim Benton

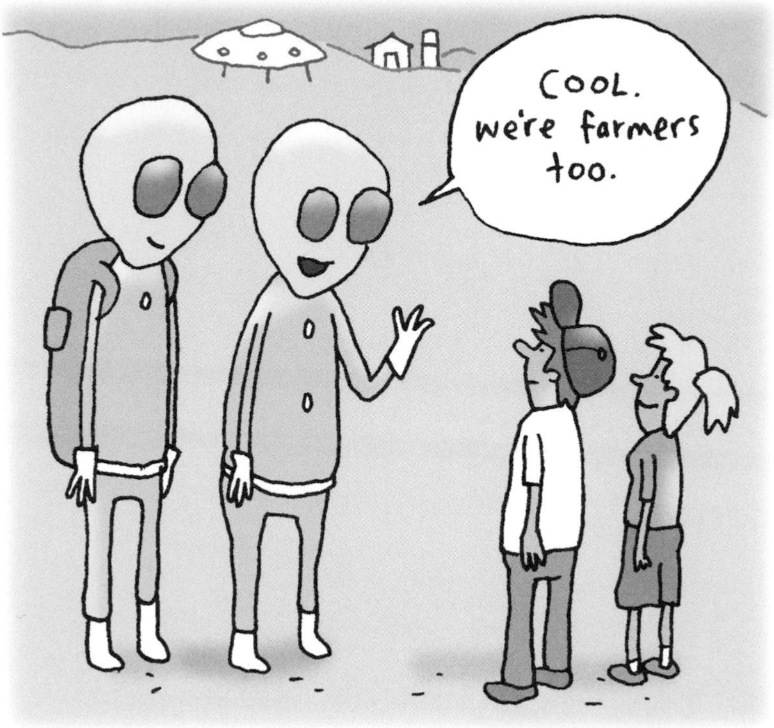
COOL. we're farmers too.

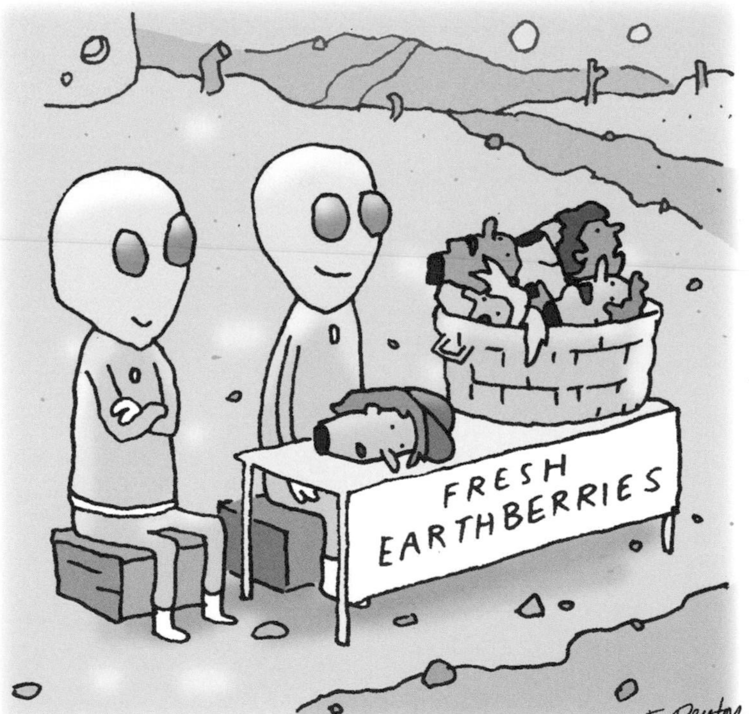
FRESH EARTHBERRIES
©Jim Benton

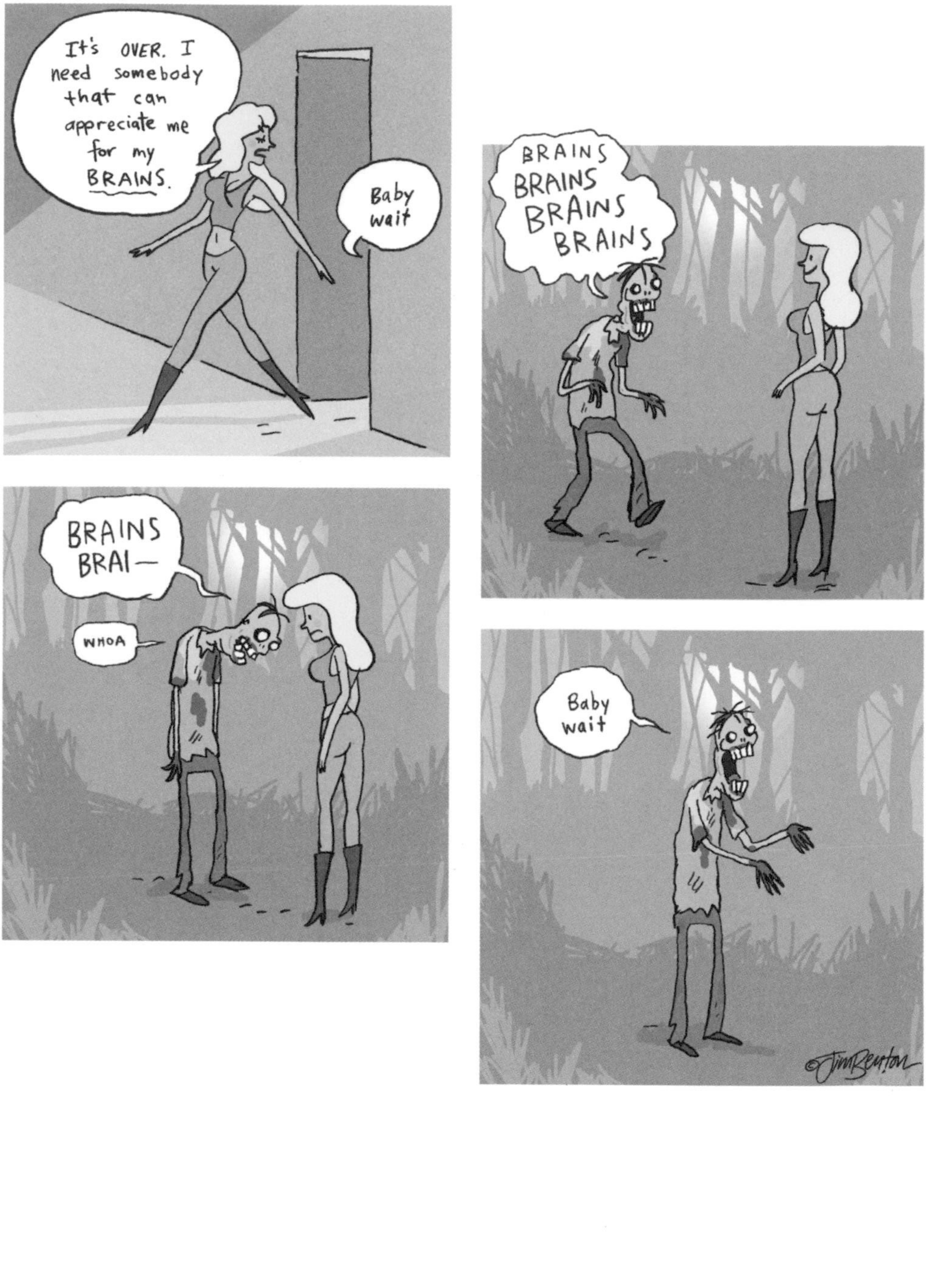
It's OVER. I need somebody that can appreciate me for my BRAINS.
Baby wait
BRAINS BRAINS BRAINS BRAINS
BRAINS BRAI—
WHOA
Baby wait
©Jim Benton

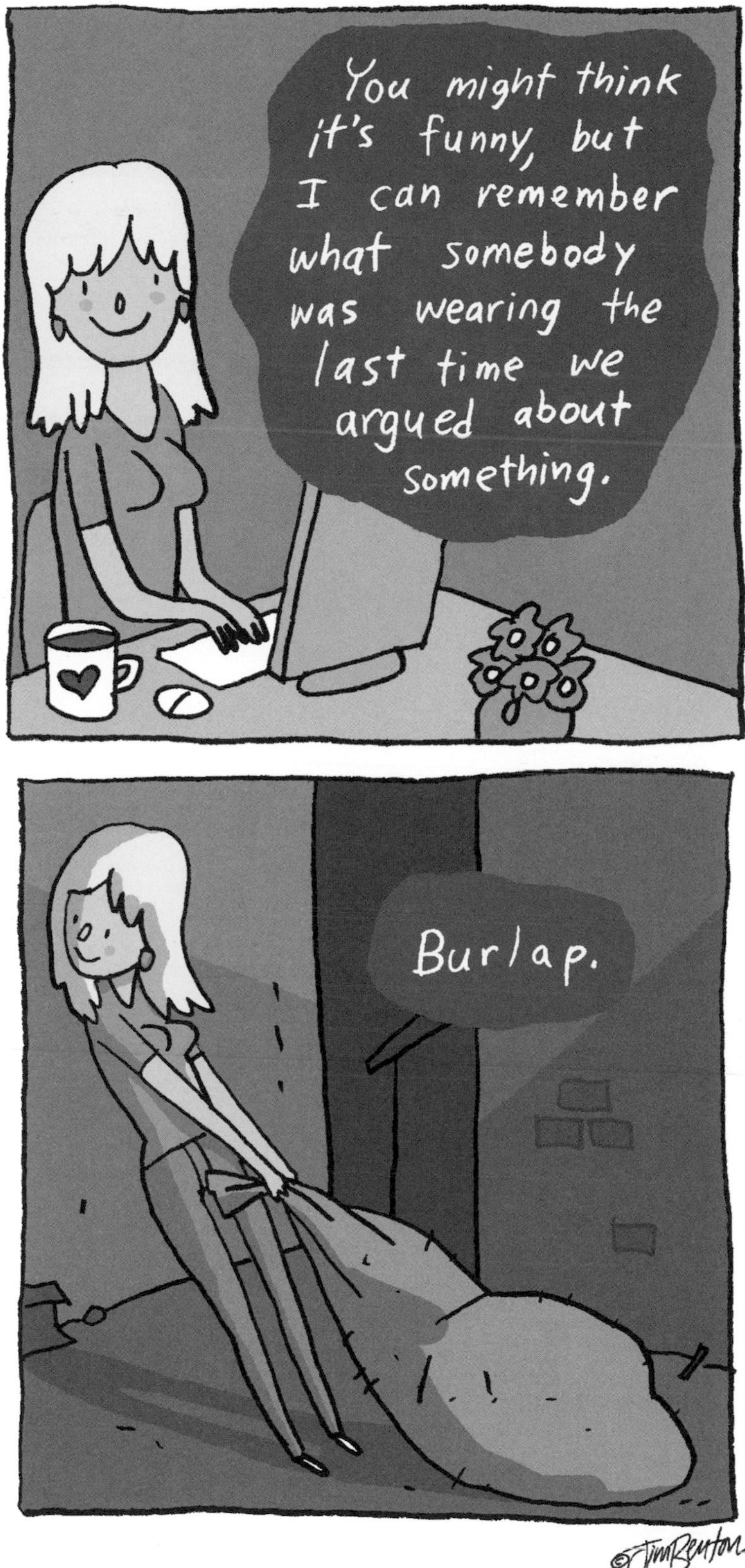
You might think it's funny, but I can remember what somebody was wearing the last time we argued about something.
Burlap.
©Jim Benton

WHAT IS *BUSINESS CASUAL?*

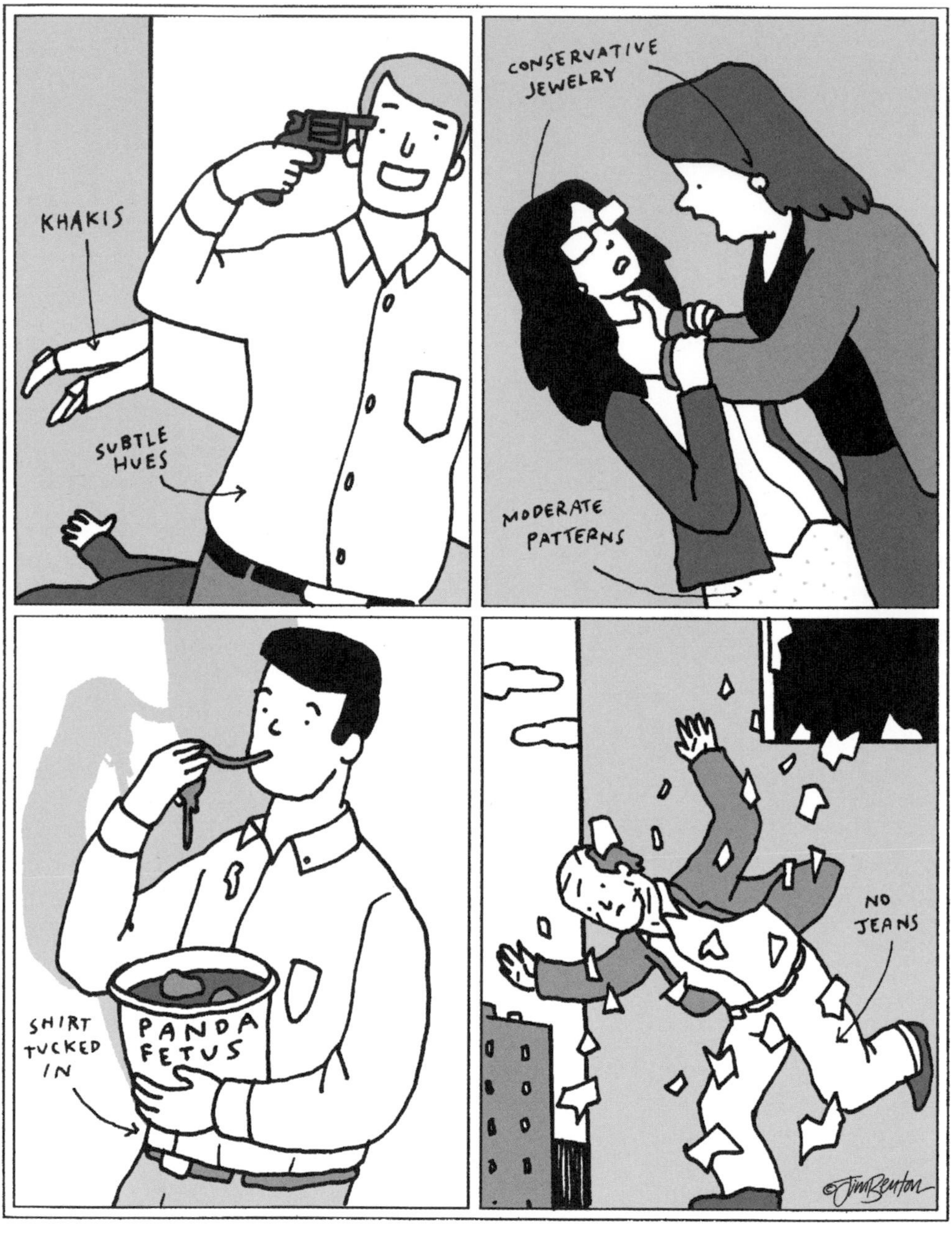

KHAKIS
SUBTLE HUES
CONSERVATIVE JEWELRY
MODERATE PATTERNS
SHIRT TUCKED IN
PANDA FETUS
NO JEANS
©JimBenton

THE COSMIC ADJUSTER

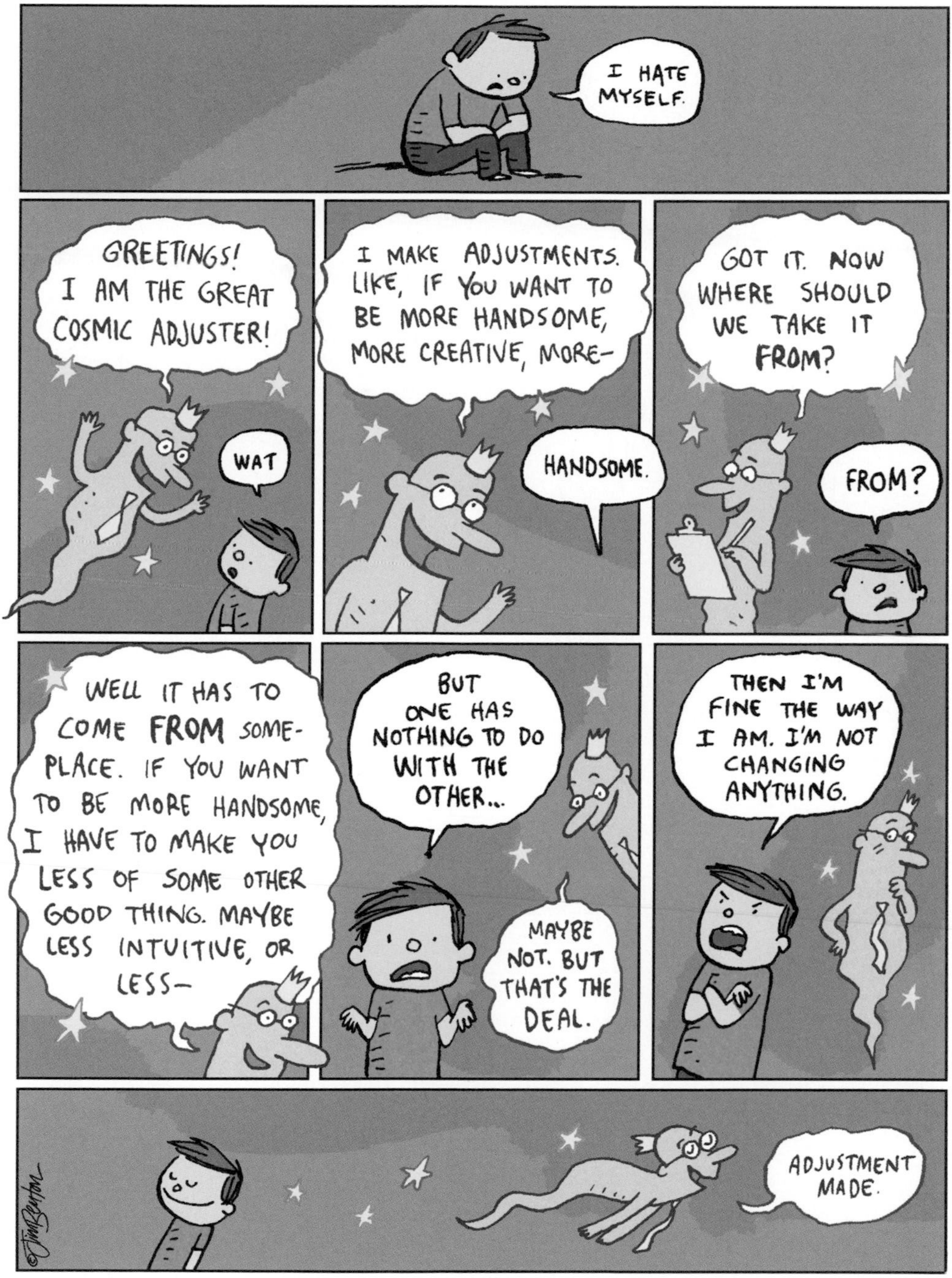
I HATE MYSELF.
GREETINGS! I AM THE GREAT COSMIC ADJUSTER!
WAT
I MAKE ADJUSTMENTS. LIKE, IF YOU WANT TO BE MORE HANDSOME, MORE CREATIVE, MORE-
HANDSOME.
GOT IT. NOW WHERE SHOULD WE TAKE IT FROM?
FROM?
WELL IT HAS TO COME FROM SOME-PLACE. IF YOU WANT TO BE MORE HANDSOME, I HAVE TO MAKE YOU LESS OF SOME OTHER GOOD THING. MAYBE LESS INTUITIVE, OR LESS-
BUT ONE HAS NOTHING TO DO WITH THE OTHER...
MAYBE NOT. BUT THAT'S THE DEAL.
THEN I'M FINE THE WAY I AM. I'M NOT CHANGING ANYTHING.
ADJUSTMENT MADE.
©Jim Benton

©Jim Benton

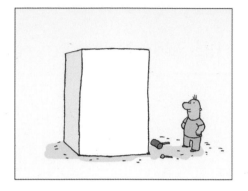

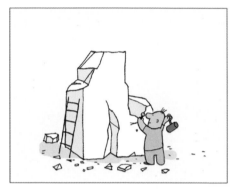

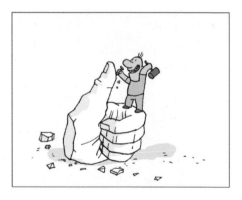

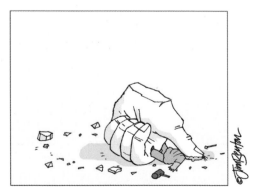

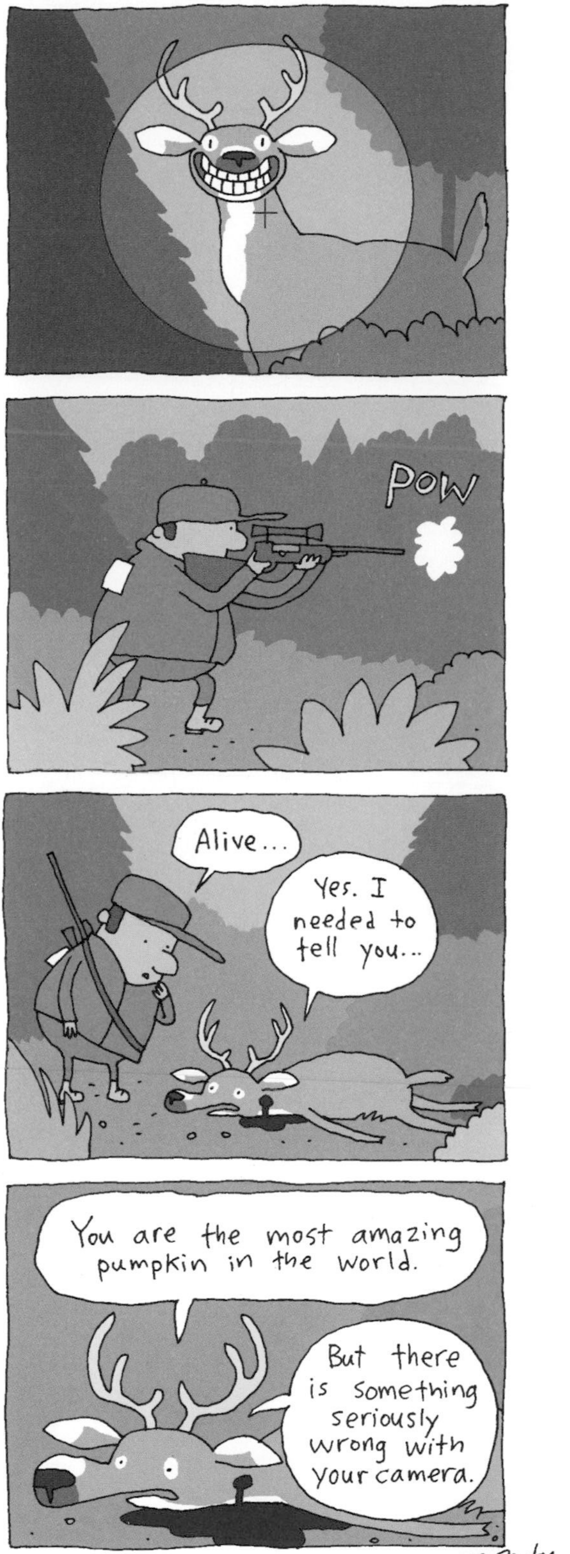
POW
Alive...
Yes. I needed to tell you...
You are the most amazing pumpkin in the world.
But there is something seriously wrong with your camera.
©Jim Benton

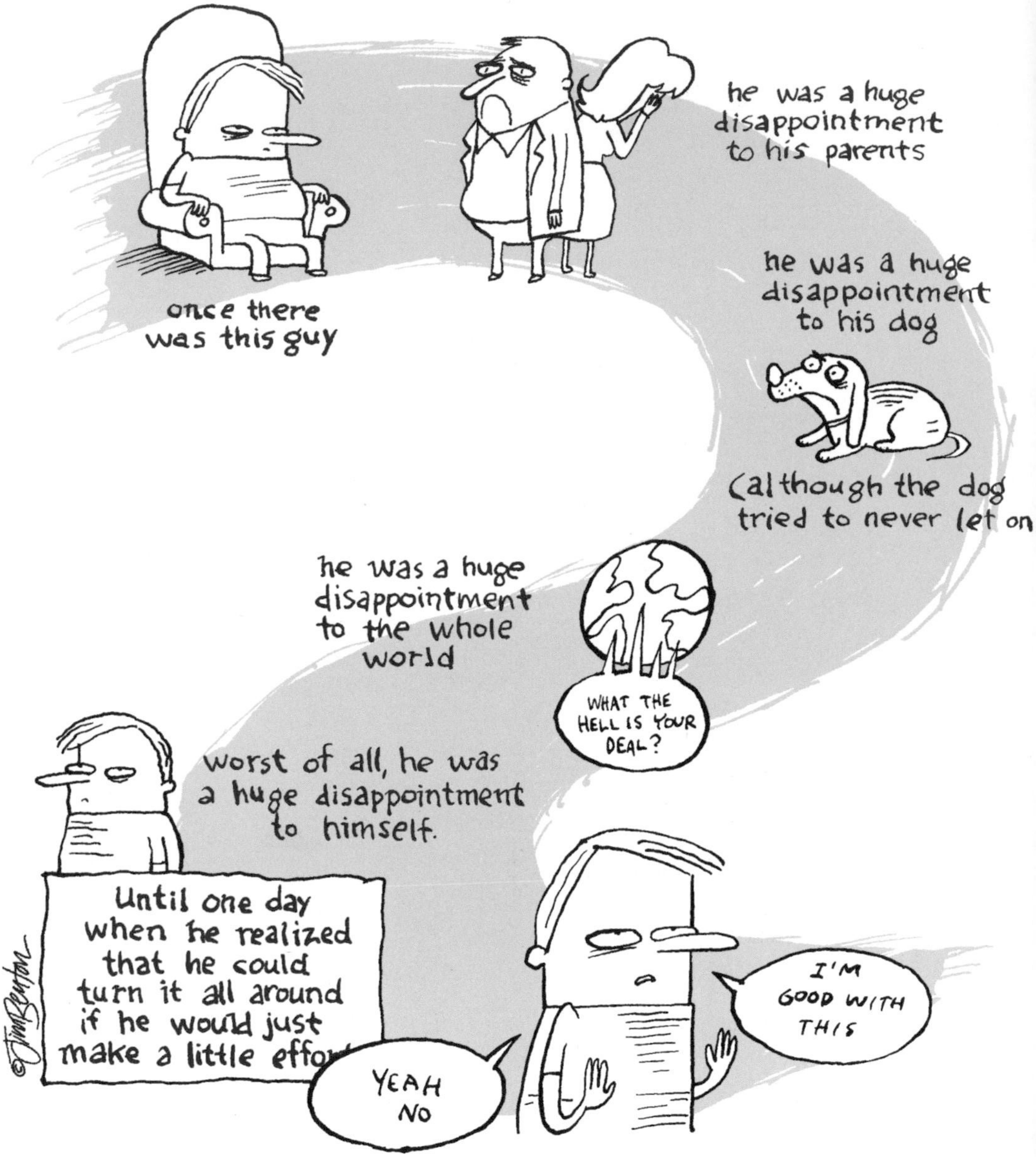
once there was this guy
he was a huge disappointment to his parents
he was a huge disappointment to his dog
(although the dog tried to never let on
he was a huge disappointment to the whole world
WHAT THE HELL IS YOUR DEAL?
worst of all, he was a huge disappointment to himself.
Until one day when he realized that he could turn it all around if he would just make a little effor
YEAH NO
I'M GOOD WITH THIS
©Jim Benton

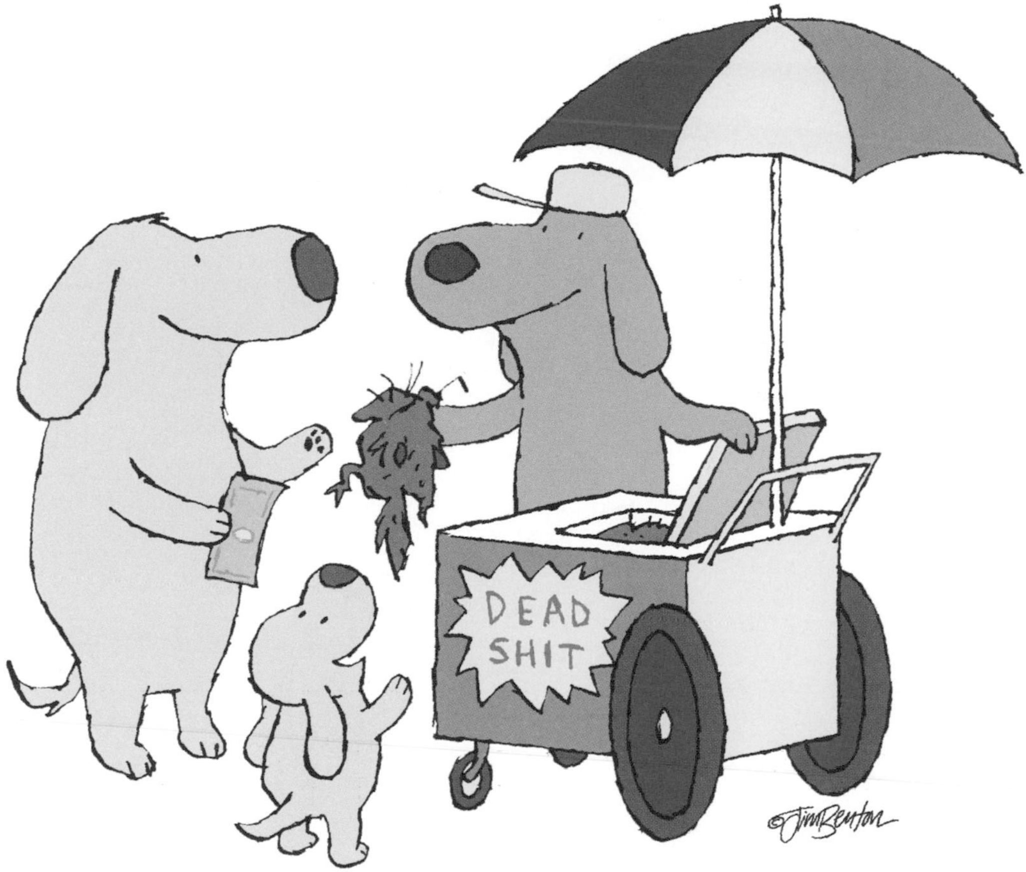
DEAD SHIT
©Jim Benton

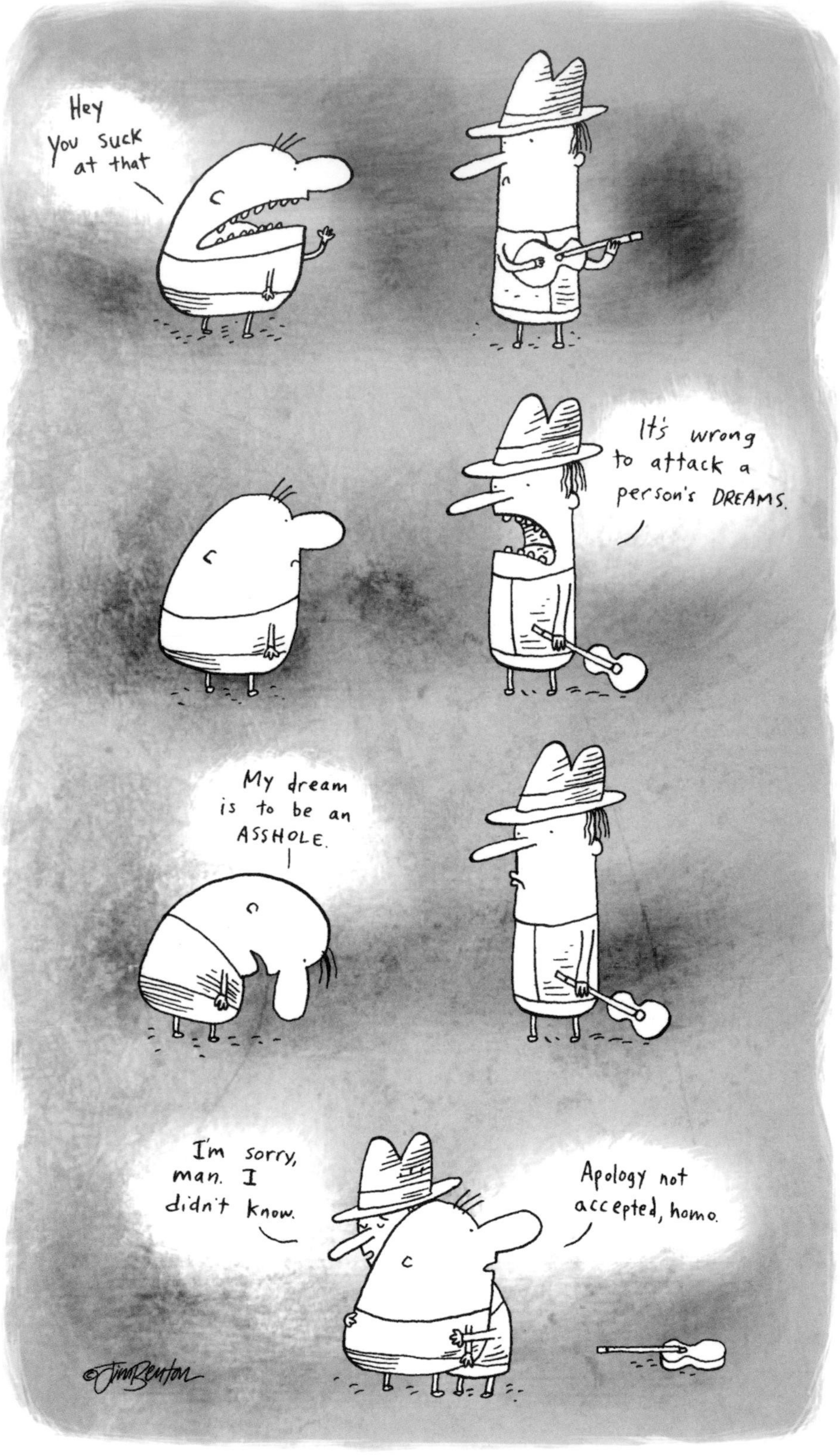
Hey you suck at that
It's wrong to attack a person's DREAMS.
My dream is to be an ASSHOLE.
I'm sorry, man. I didn't know.
Apology not accepted, homo.
©Jim Benton

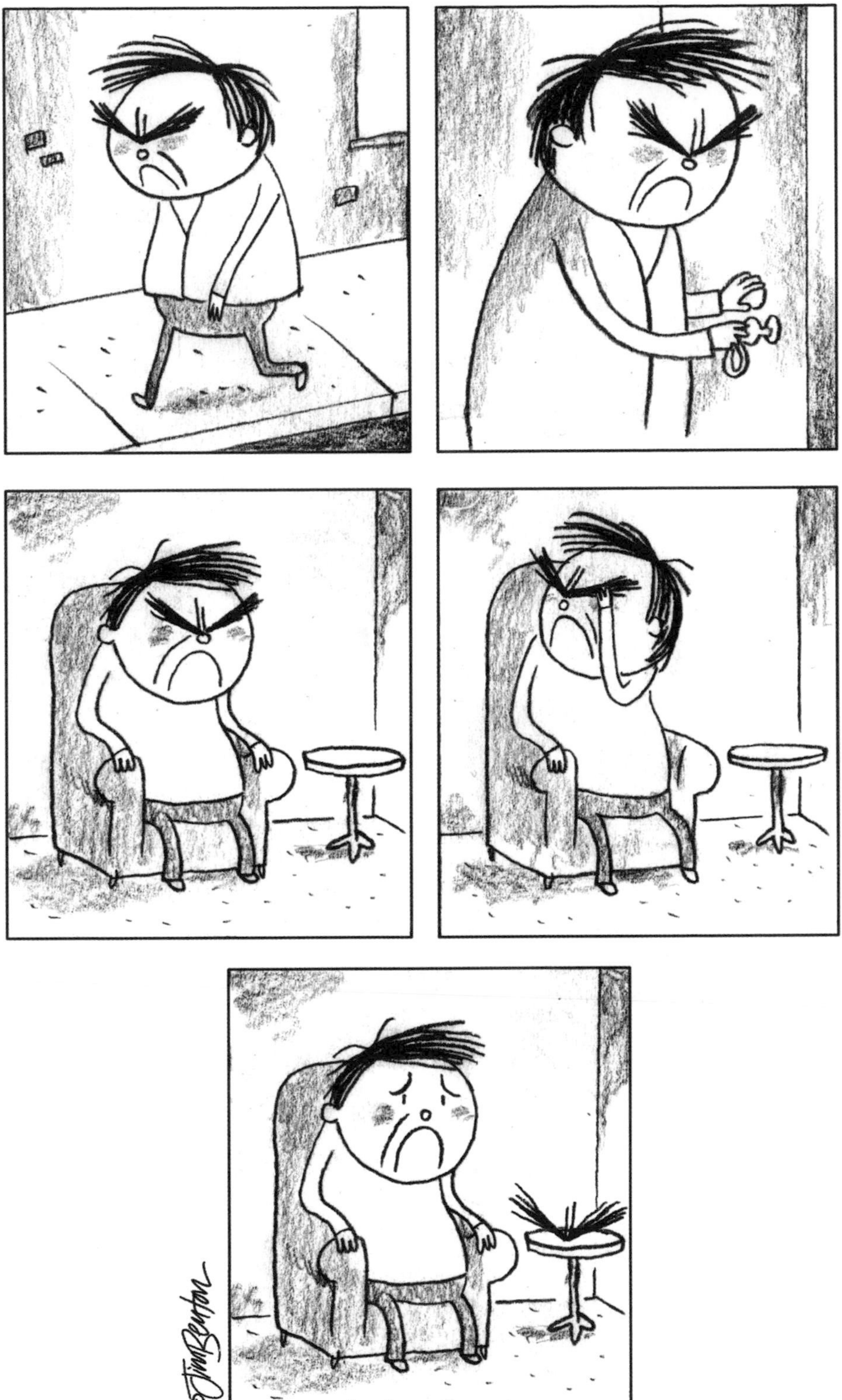
©Jim Benton

THE EASTER BUNNY

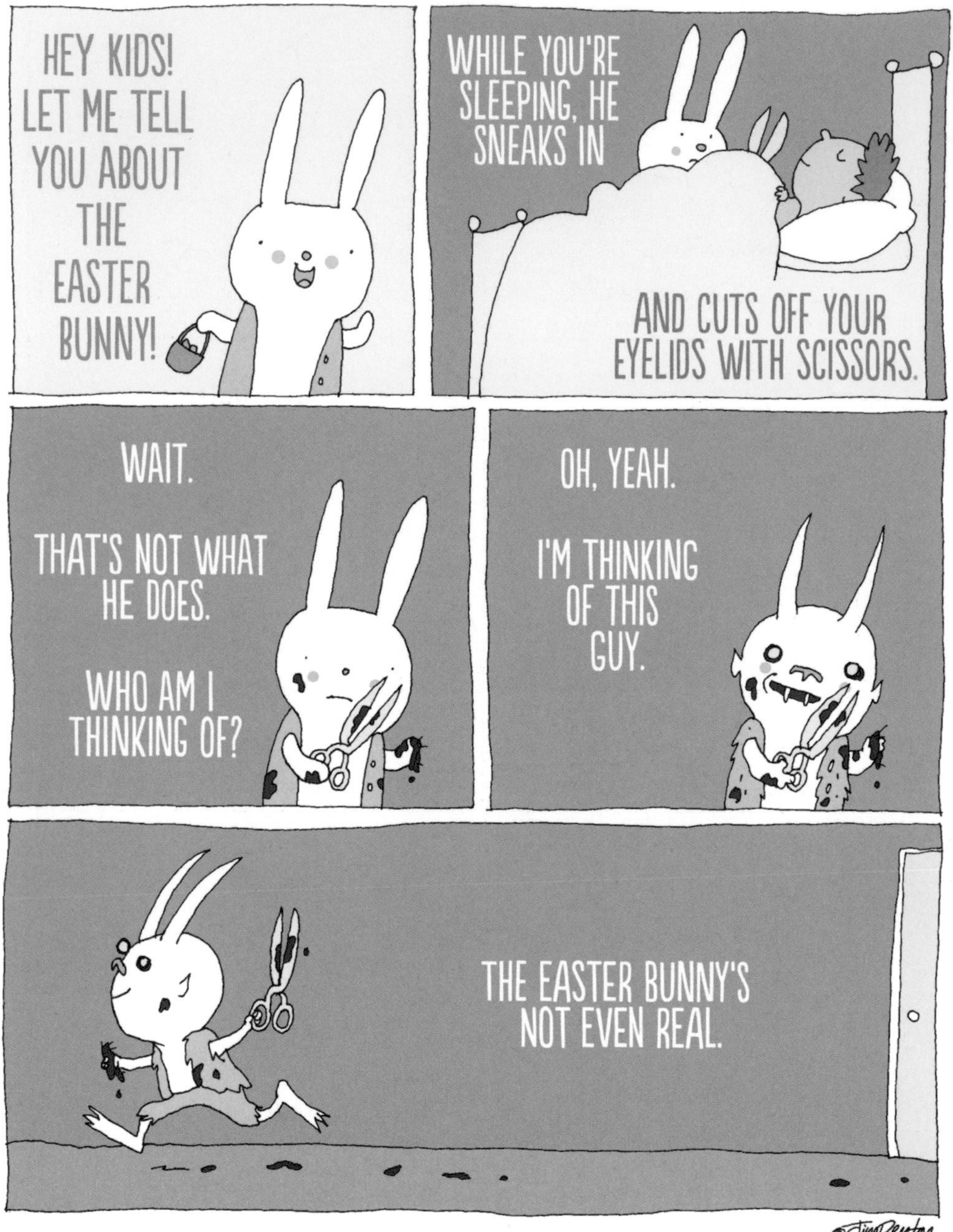
HEY KIDS! LET ME TELL YOU ABOUT THE EASTER BUNNY!
WHILE YOU'RE SLEEPING, HE SNEAKS IN
AND CUTS OFF YOUR EYELIDS WITH SCISSORS.
WAIT.
THAT'S NOT WHAT HE DOES.
WHO AM I THINKING OF?
OH, YEAH.
I'M THINKING OF THIS GUY.
THE EASTER BUNNY'S NOT EVEN REAL.

©Jim Benton

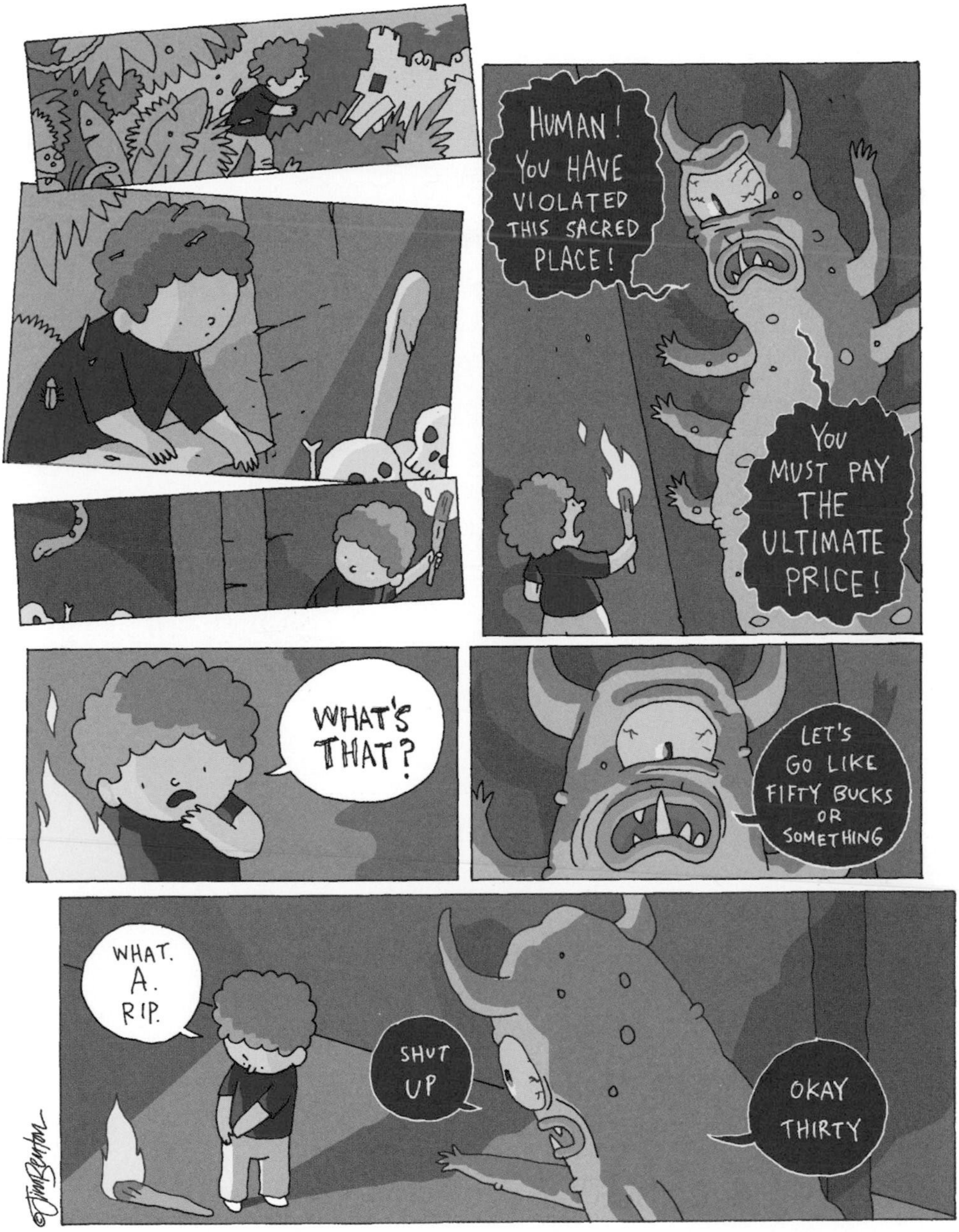
HUMAN! YOU HAVE VIOLATED THIS SACRED PLACE!
YOU MUST PAY THE ULTIMATE PRICE!
WHAT'S THAT?
LET'S GO LIKE FIFTY BUCKS OR SOMETHING
WHAT. A. RIP.
SHUT UP
OKAY THIRTY
©Jim Benton

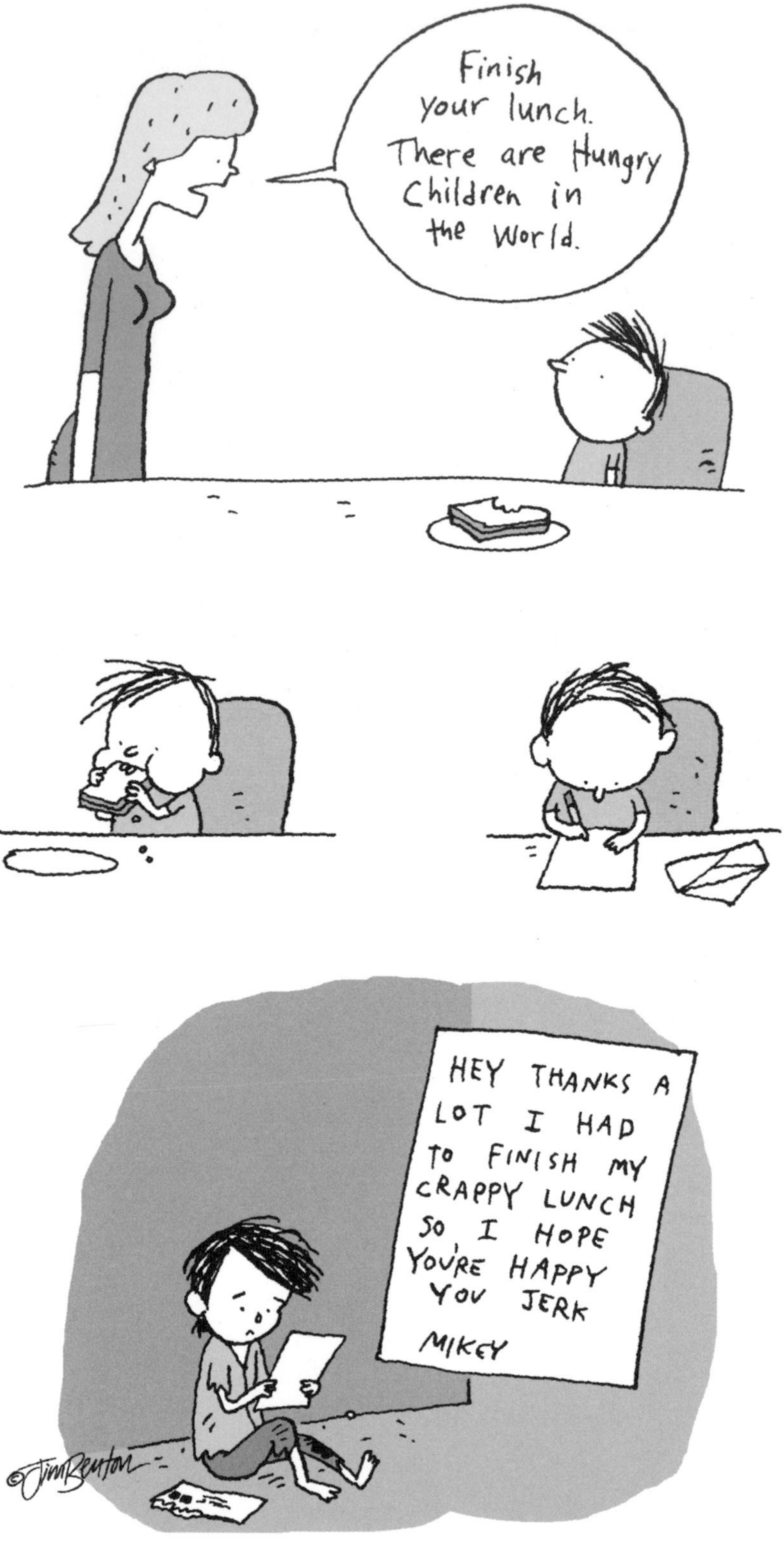
Finish your lunch. There are Hungry Children in the World.
HEY THANKS A LOT I HAD TO FINISH MY CRAPPY LUNCH SO I HOPE YOU'RE HAPPY YOU JERK
MIKEY
©JimBenton

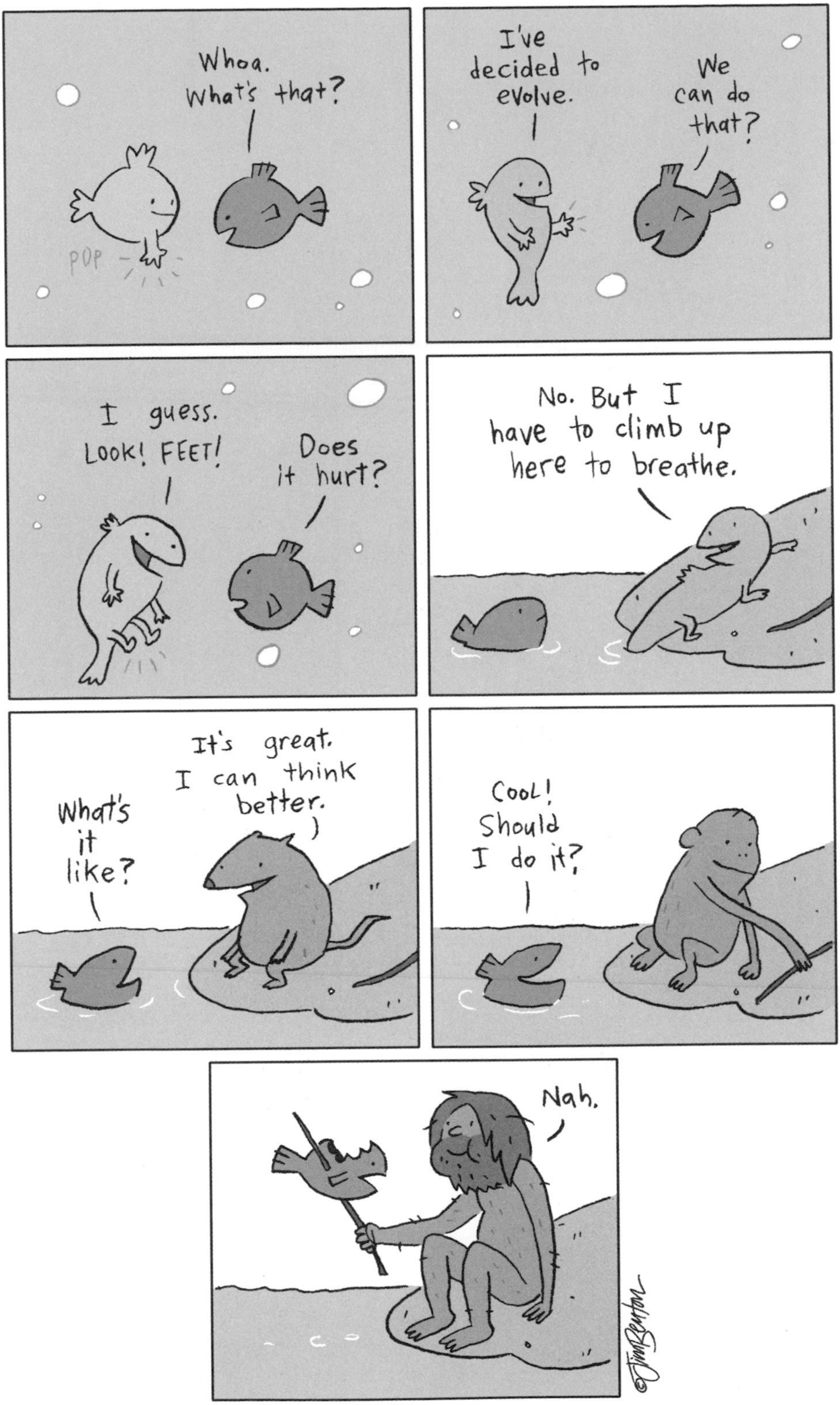
POP
Whoa. What's that?
I've decided to evolve.
We can do that?
I guess. LOOK! FEET!
Does it hurt?
No. But I have to climb up here to breathe.
What's it like?
It's great. I can think better.
Cool! Should I do it?
Nah.
©Jim Benton

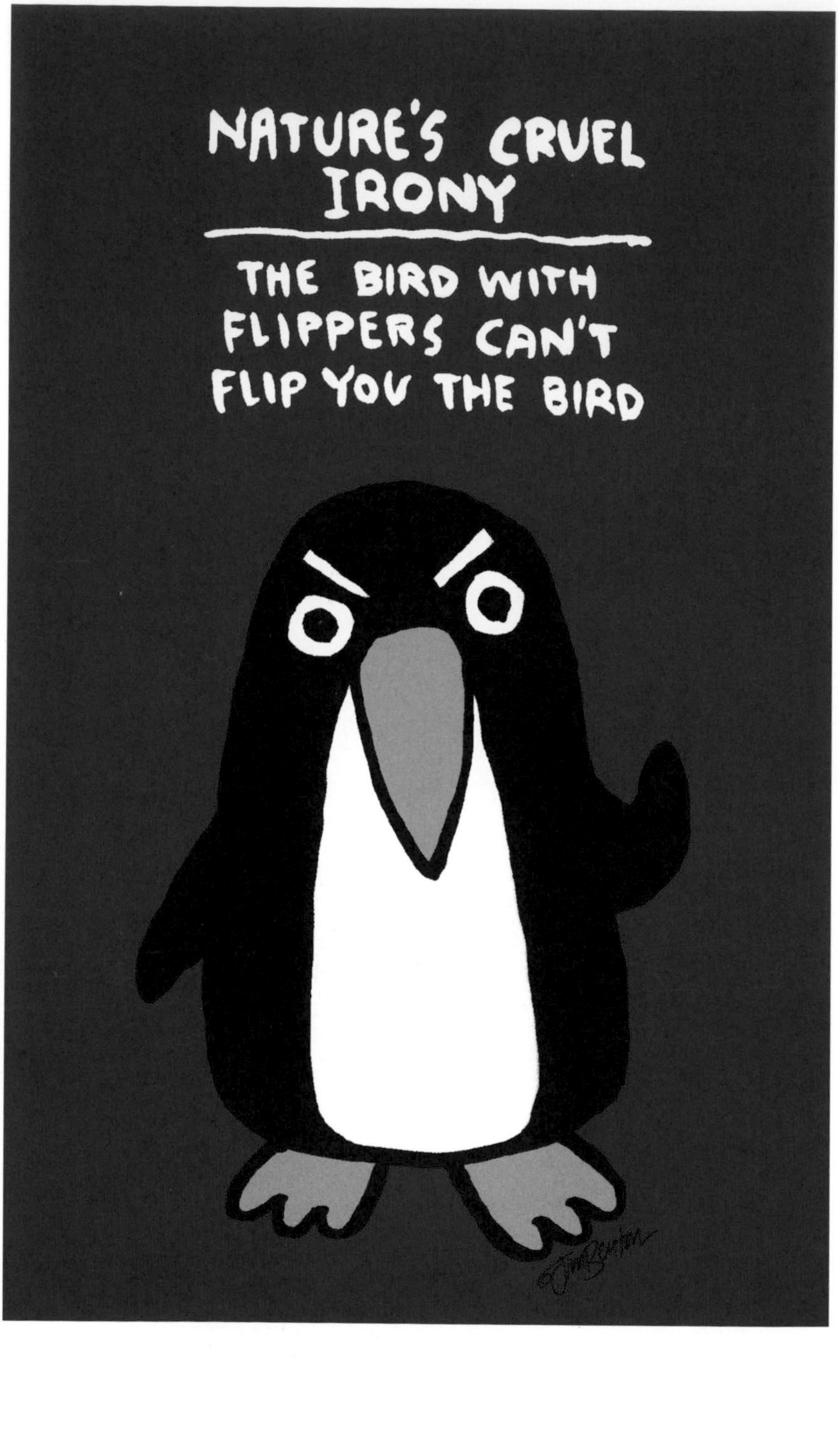
NATURE'S CRUEL IRONY
THE BIRD WITH FLIPPERS CAN'T FLIP YOU THE BIRD

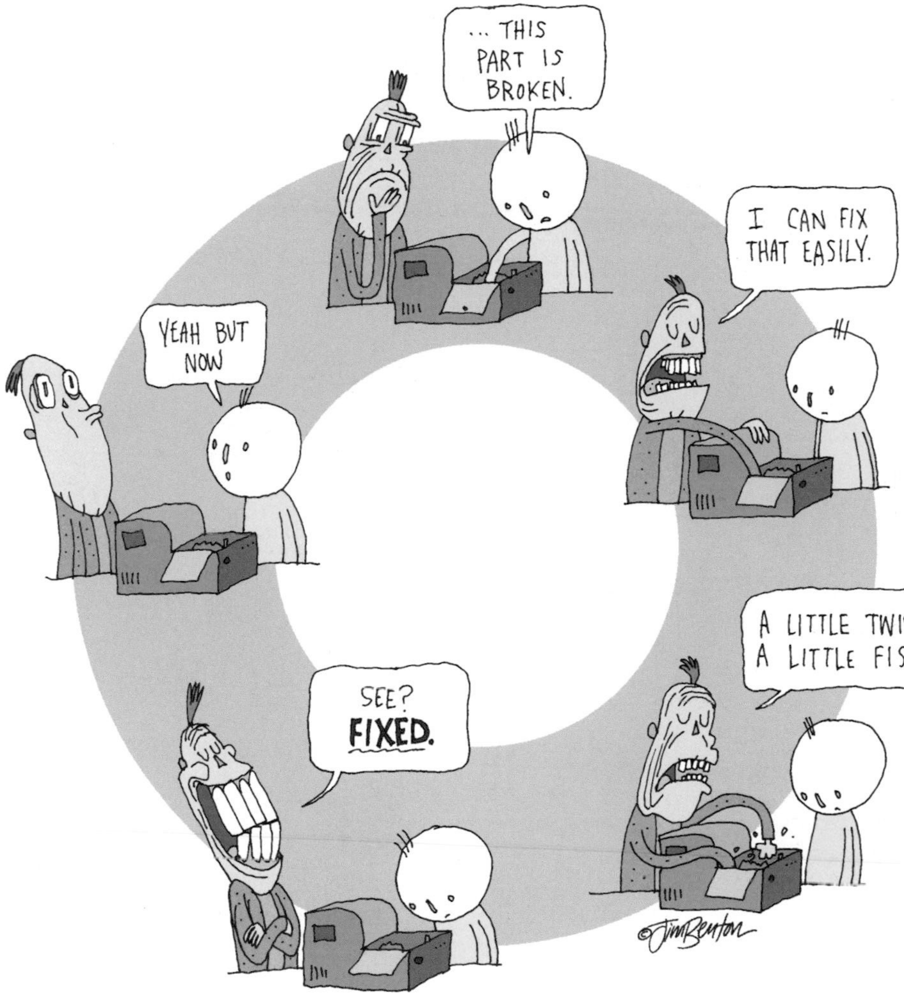
... THIS PART IS BROKEN.
I CAN FIX THAT EASILY.
A LITTLE TWIST, A LITTLE FIST...
SEE? FIXED.
YEAH BUT NOW
©Jim Benton

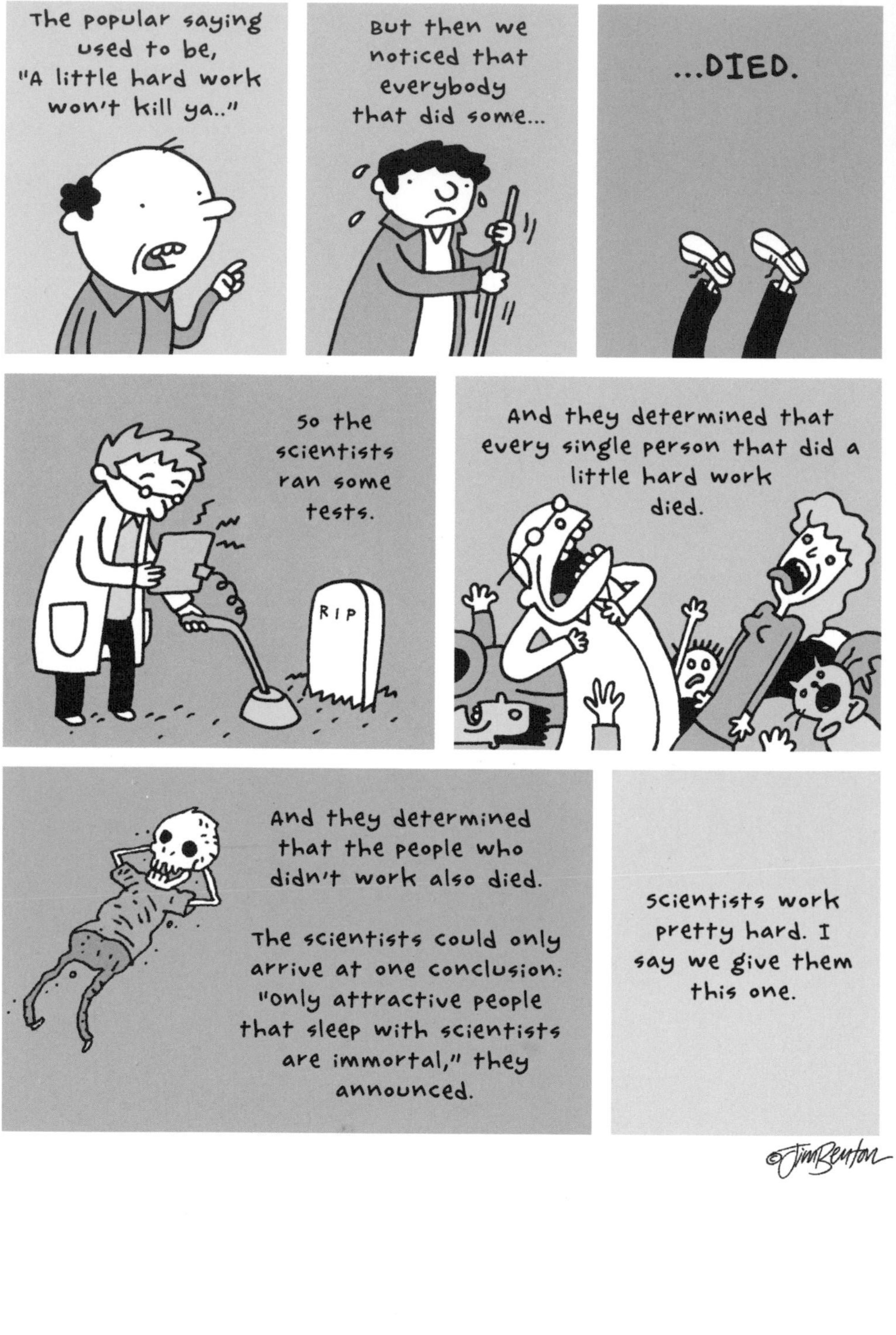

The popular saying used to be, "A little hard work won't kill ya.."
But then we noticed that everybody that did some...
...DIED.
So the scientists ran some tests.
RIP
And they determined that every single person that did a little hard work died.
And they determined that the people who didn't work also died.
The scientists could only arrive at one conclusion: "Only attractive people that sleep with scientists are immortal," they announced.
Scientists work pretty hard. I say we give them this one.
©Jim Benton

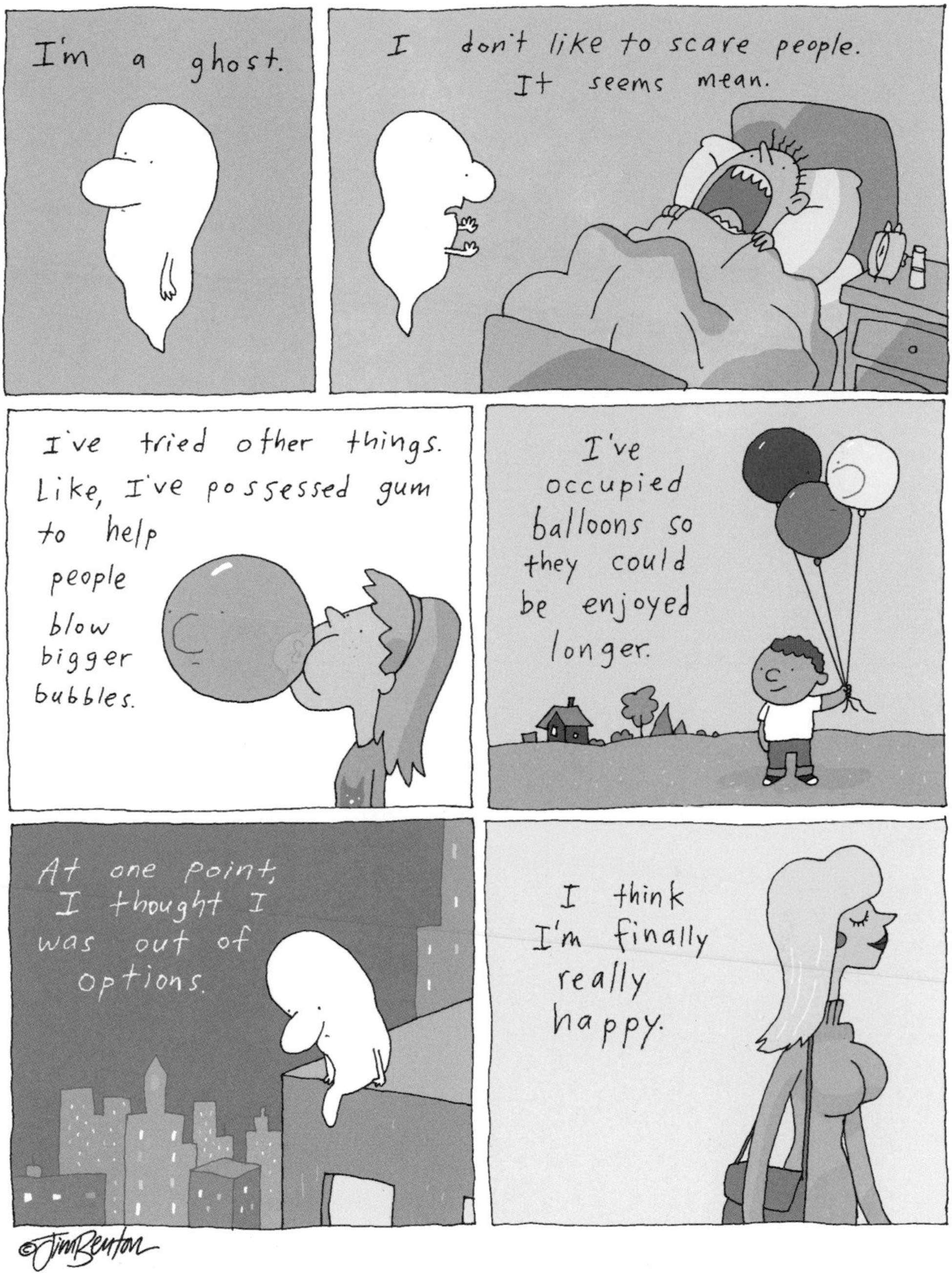
I'm a ghost.
I don't like to scare people. It seems mean.
I've tried other things. Like, I've possessed gum to help people blow bigger bubbles.
I've occupied balloons so they could be enjoyed longer.
At one point, I thought I was out of options.
I think I'm finally really happy.
©Jim Benton

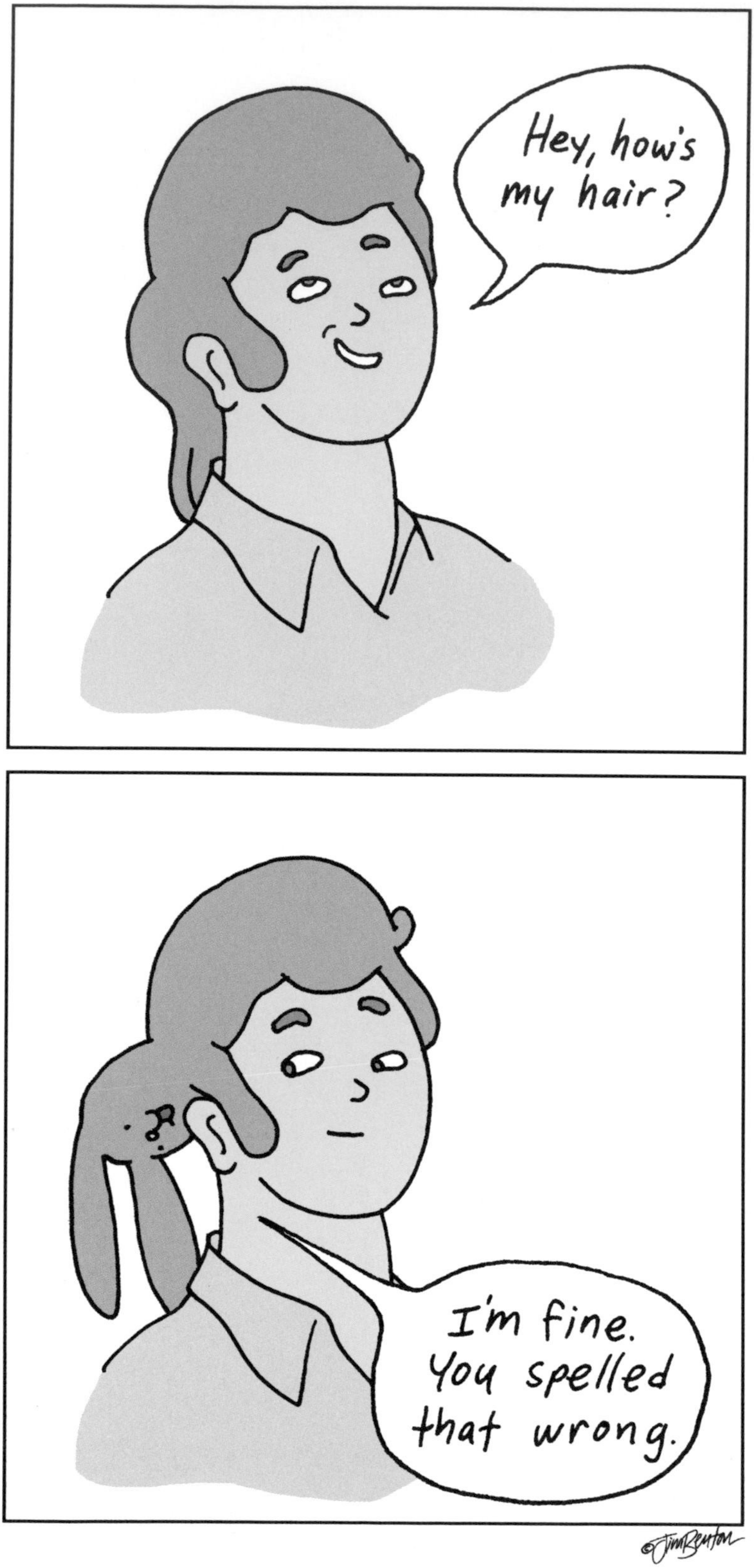
Hey, how's my hair?
I'm fine. You spelled that wrong.
©Jim Benton

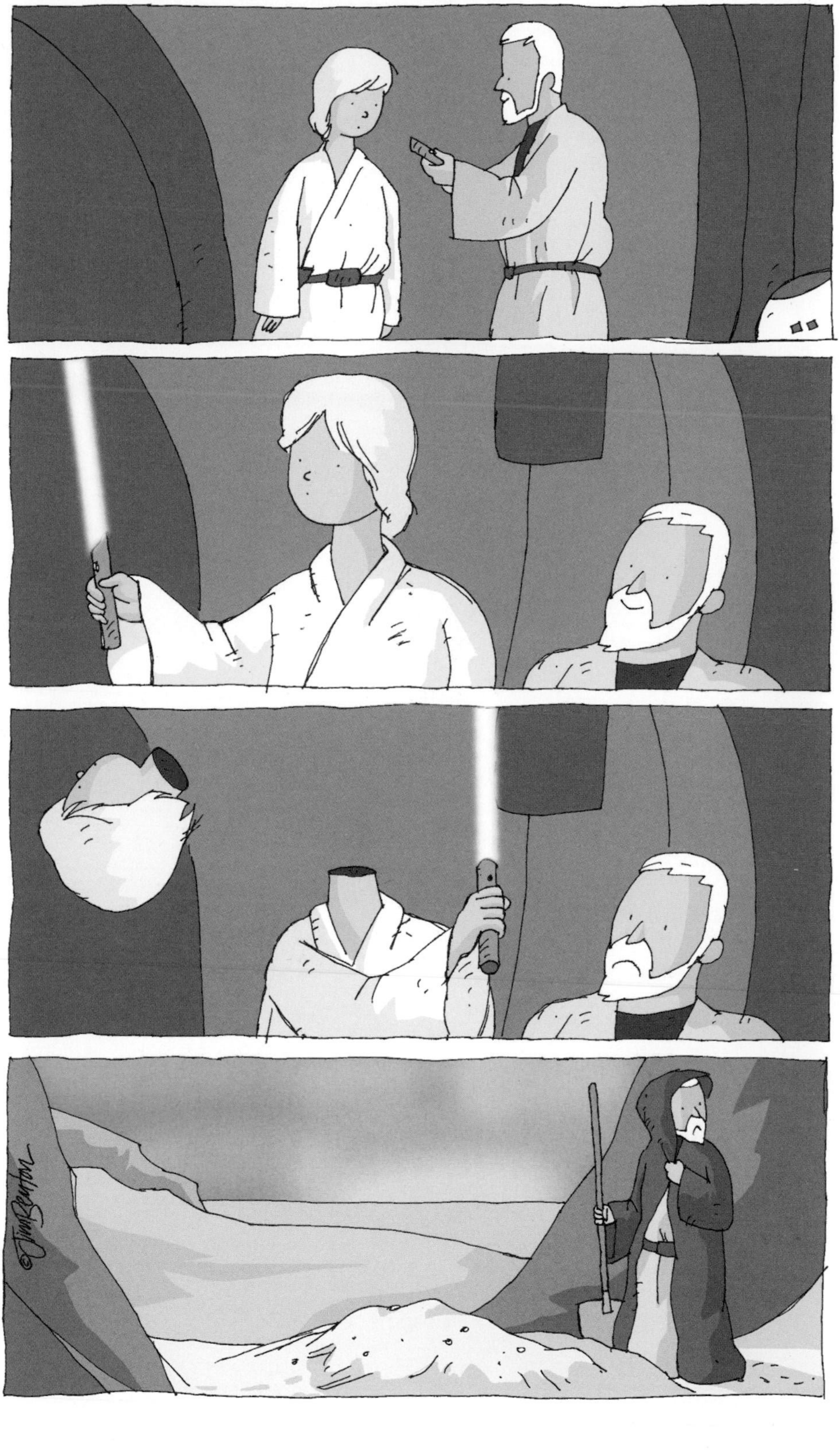
©Jim Benton

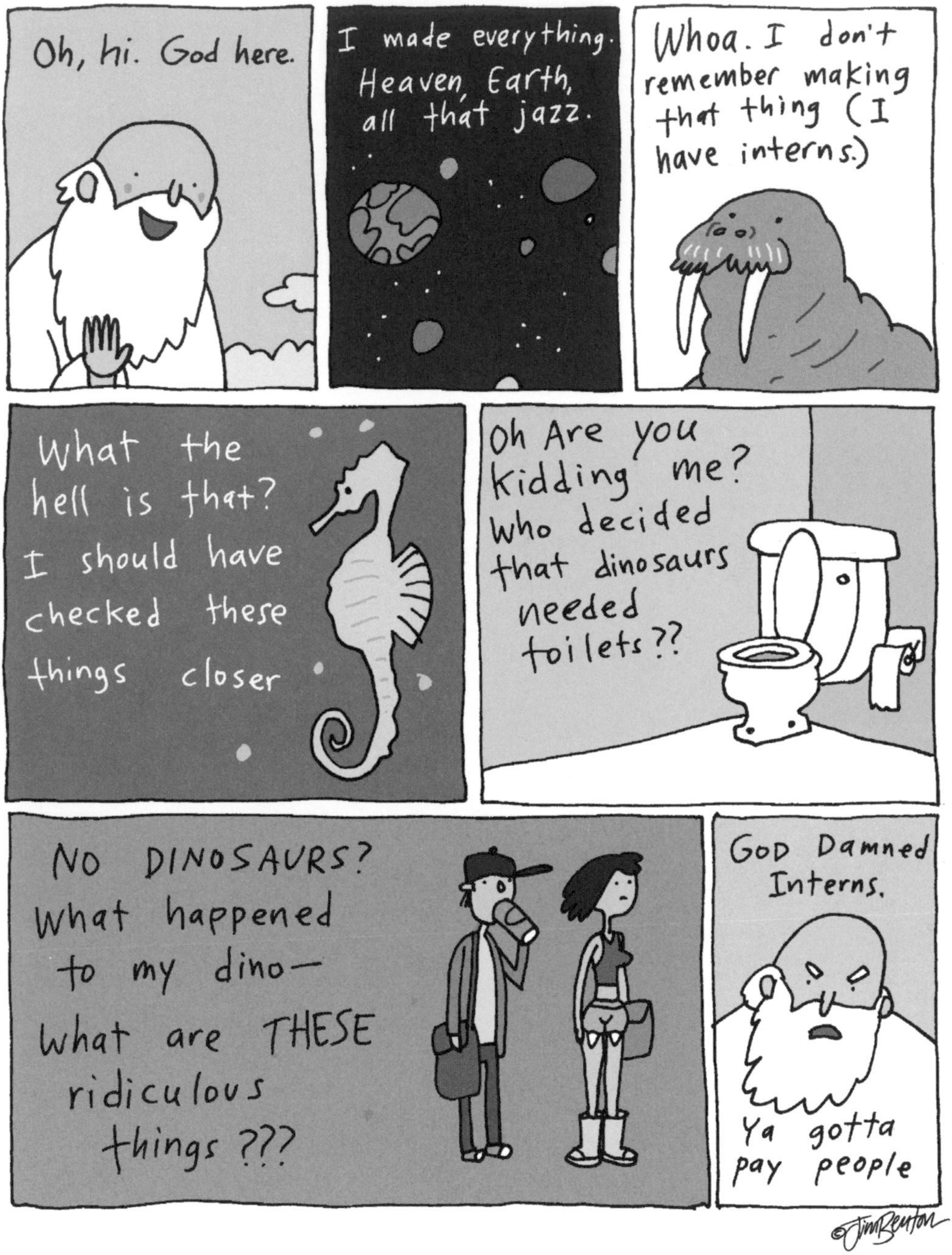
Oh, hi. God here.
I made everything. Heaven, Earth, all that jazz.
Whoa. I don't remember making that thing (I have interns.)
What the hell is that? I should have checked these things closer
Oh Are you kidding me? Who decided that dinosaurs needed toilets??
NO DINOSAURS? What happened to my dino— What are THESE ridiculous things???
GOD Damned Interns.
Ya gotta pay people
©Jim Benton

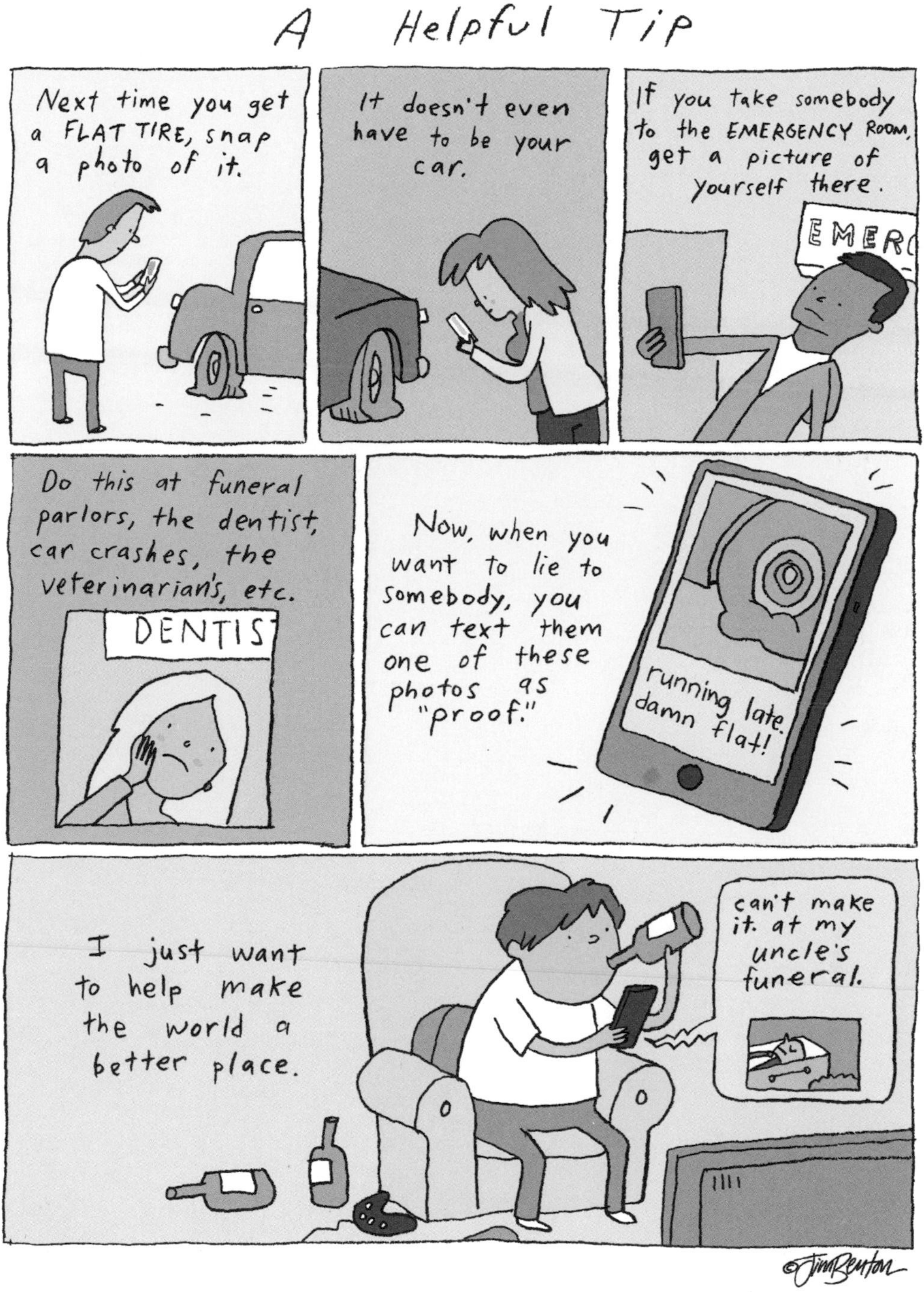
A Helpful Tip
Next time you get a FLAT TIRE, snap a photo of it.
It doesn't even have to be your car.
If you take somebody to the EMERGENCY ROOM, get a picture of yourself there.
EMERG
Do this at funeral parlors, the dentist, car crashes, the veterinarian's, etc.
DENTIS
Now, when you want to lie to somebody, you can text them one of these photos as "proof."
running late. damn flat!
I just want to help make the world a better place.
can't make it. at my uncle's funeral.
©Jim Benton

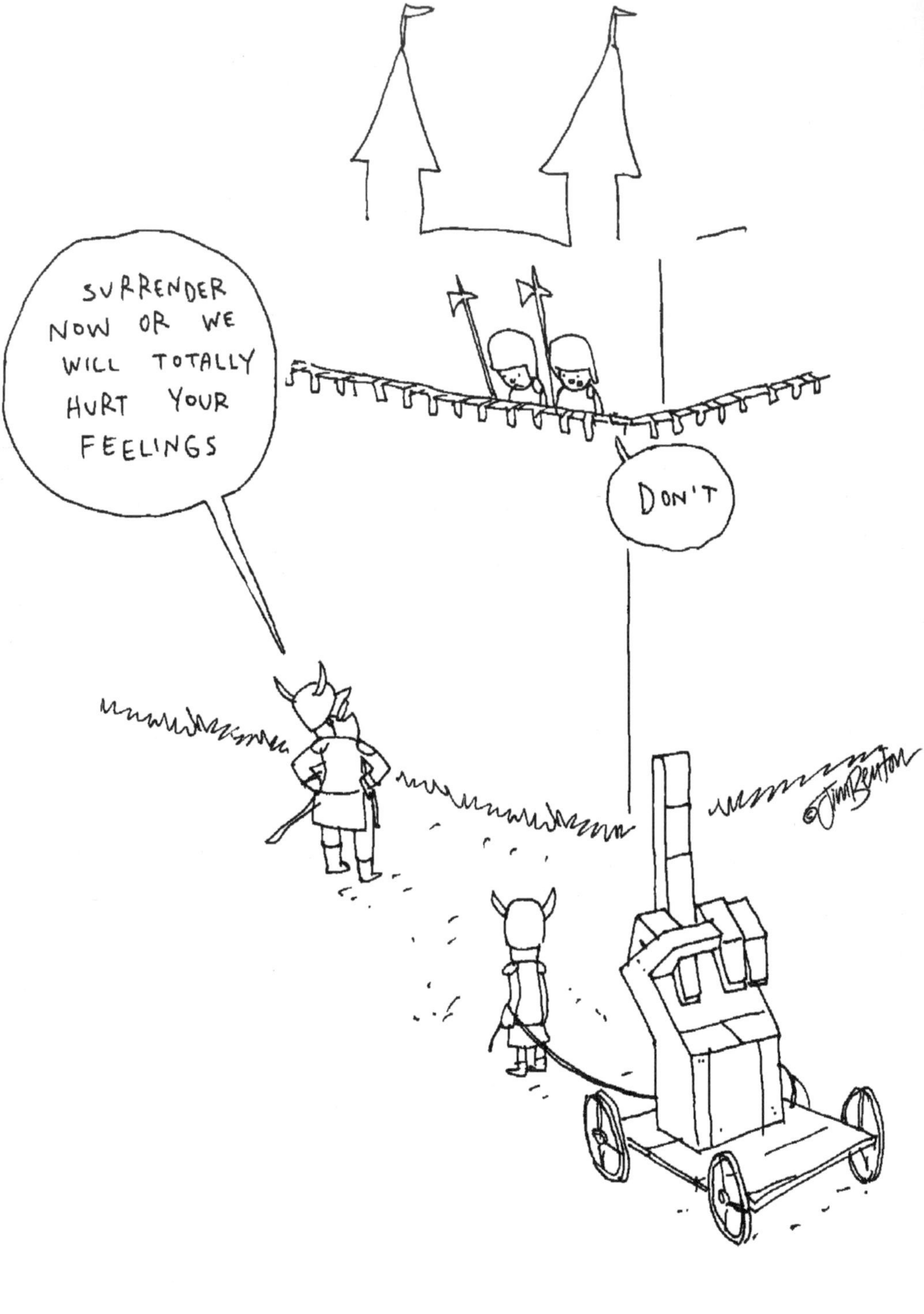
SURRENDER NOW OR WE WILL TOTALLY HURT YOUR FEELINGS
DON'T
©JimBenton

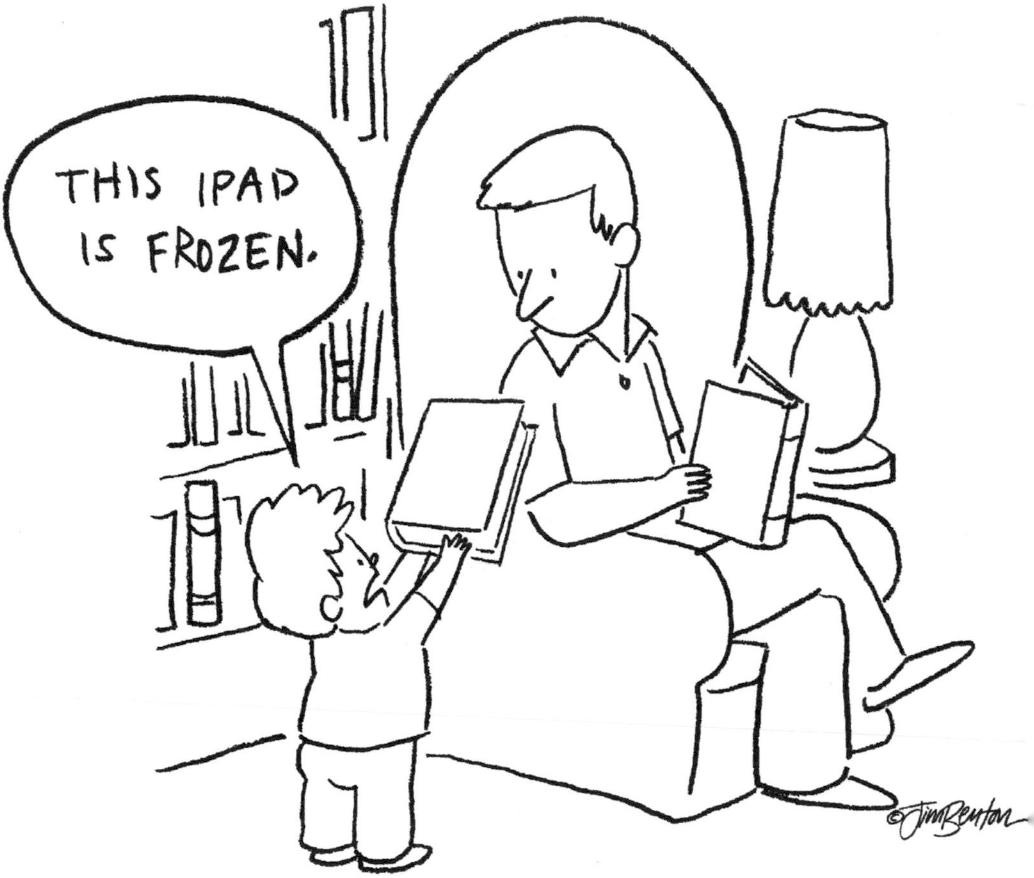
THIS IPAD IS FROZEN.
©Jim Benton

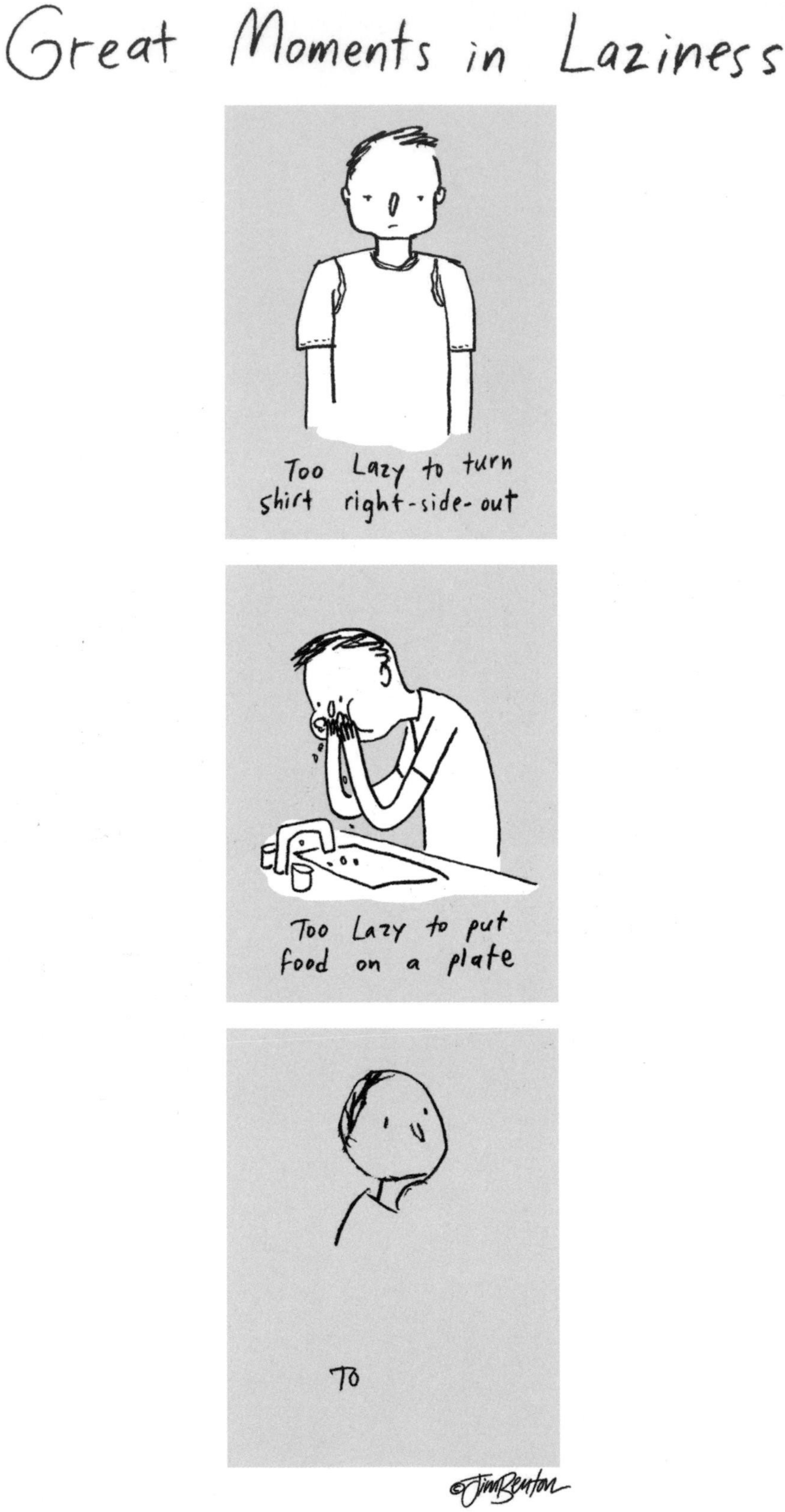
Great Moments in Laziness
Too Lazy to turn shirt right-side-out
Too Lazy to put food on a plate
TO
©Jim Benton

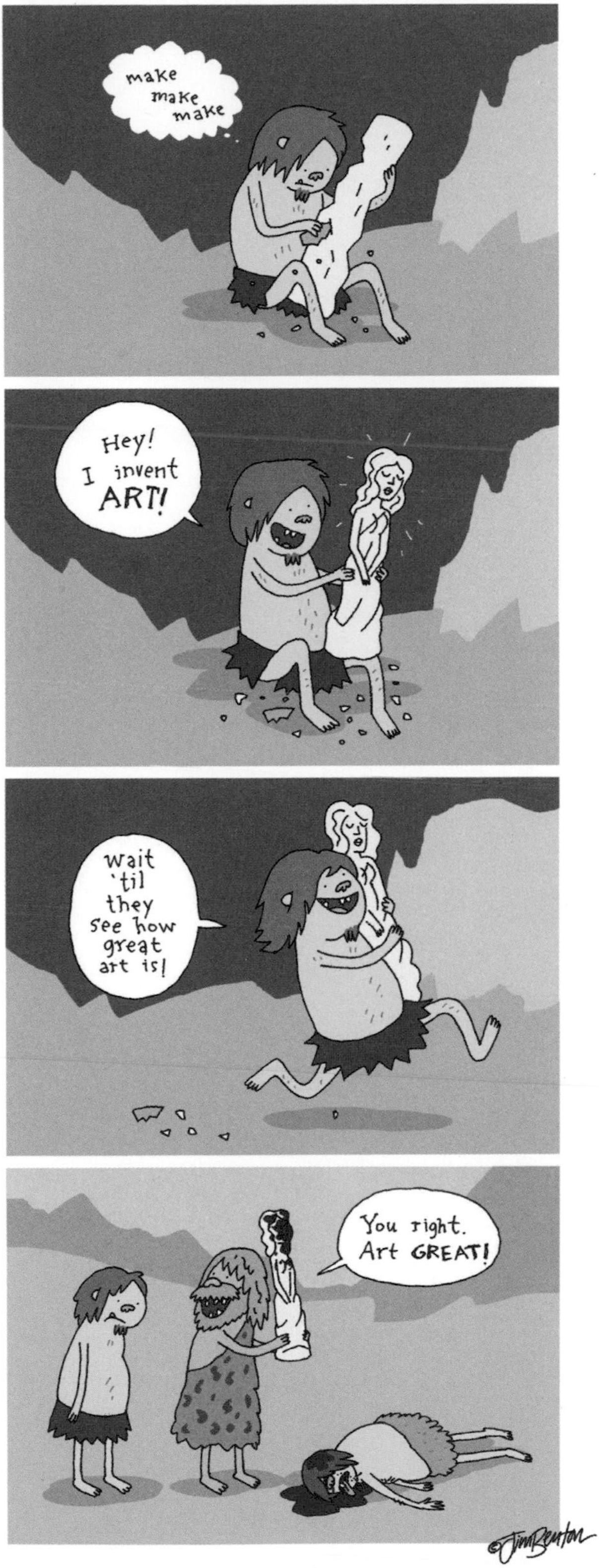
make make make
Hey! I invent ART!
wait 'til they see how great art is!
You right. Art GREAT!
©Jim Benton

How to explain things to the stupid.

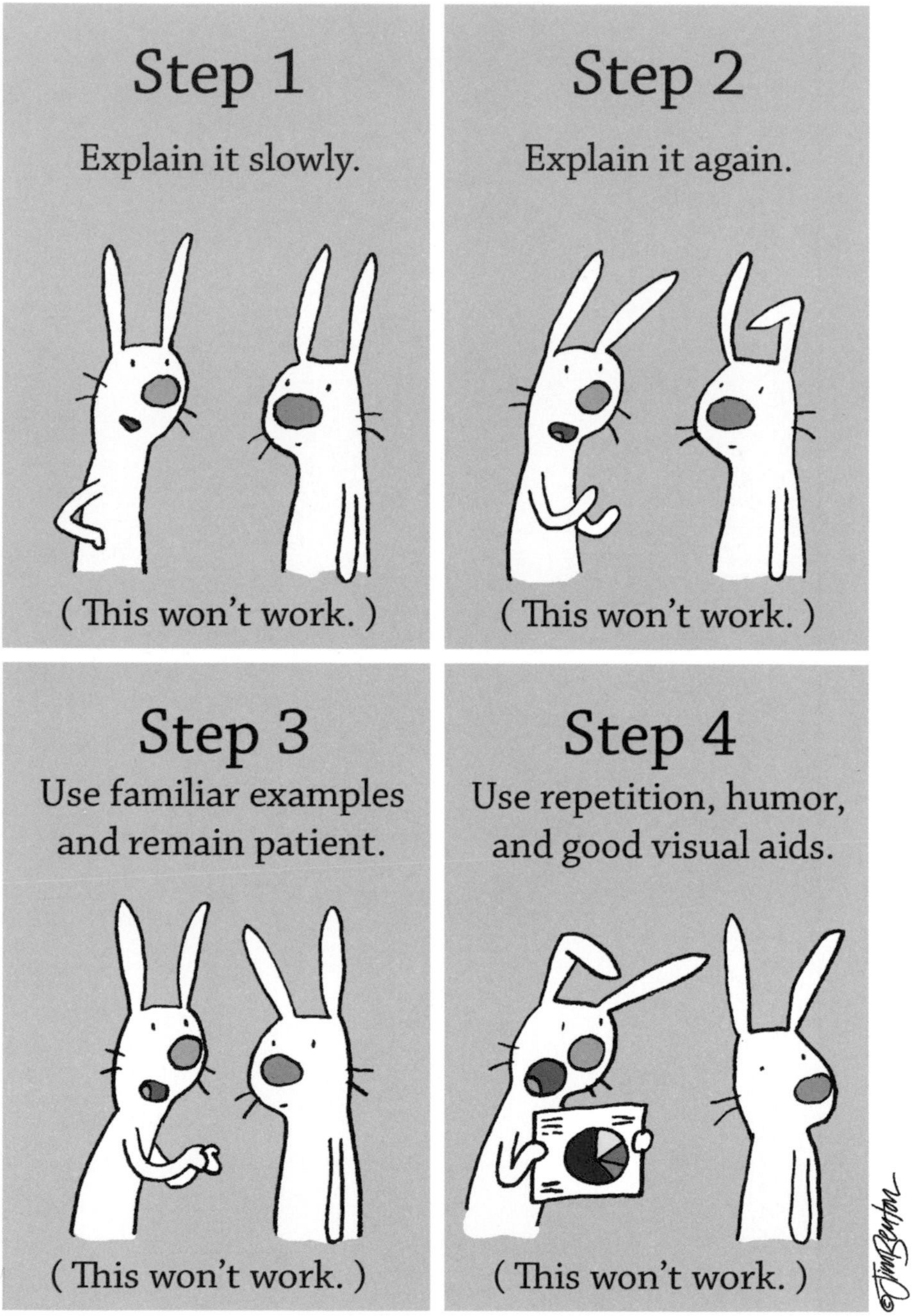
Step 1
Explain it slowly.
(This won't work.)
Step 2
Explain it again.
(This won't work.)
Step 3
Use familiar examples and remain patient.
(This won't work.)
Step 4
Use repetition, humor, and good visual aids.
(This won't work.)

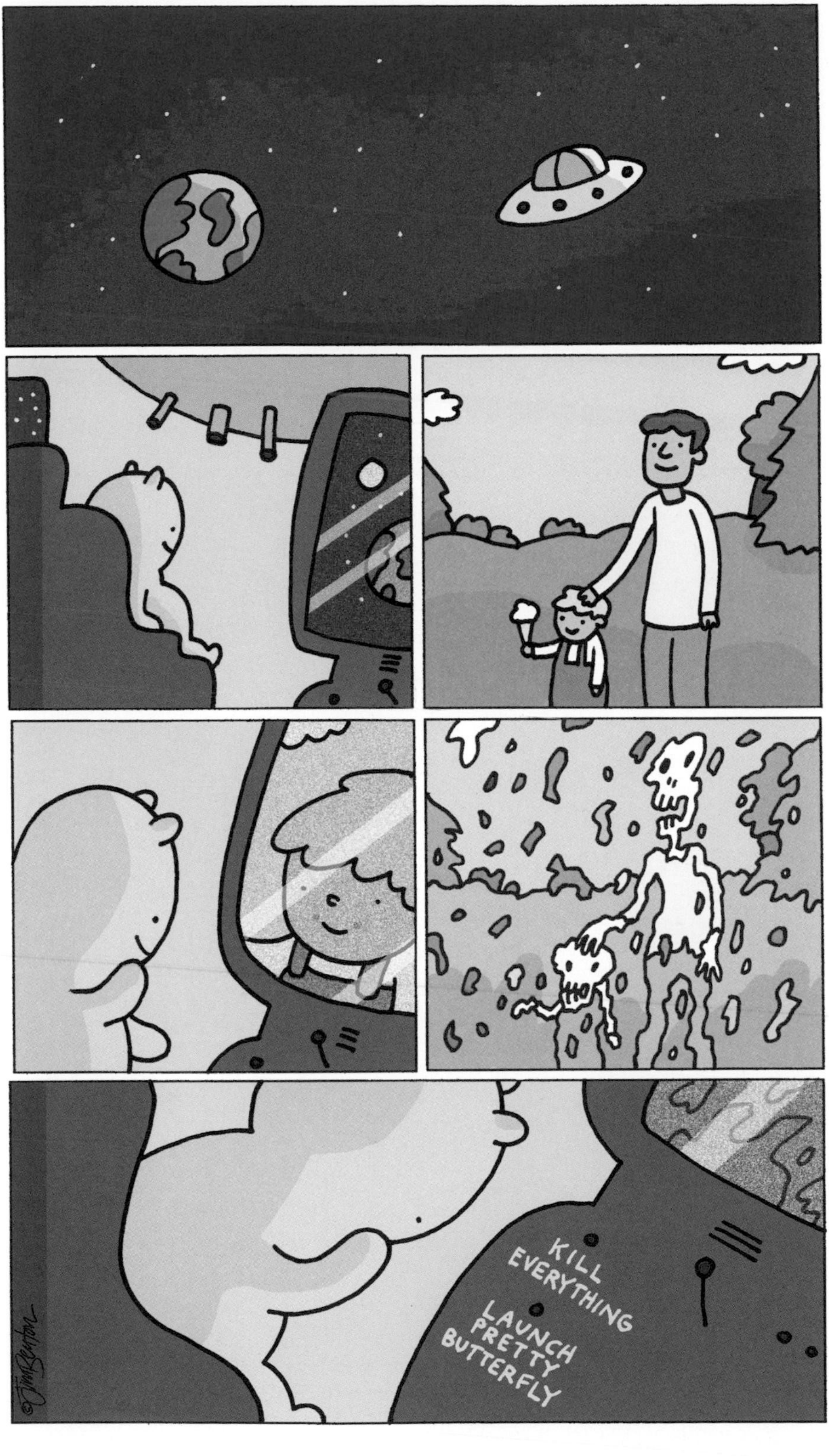
KILL EVERYTHING
LAUNCH PRETTY BUTTERFLY
© Jim Benton

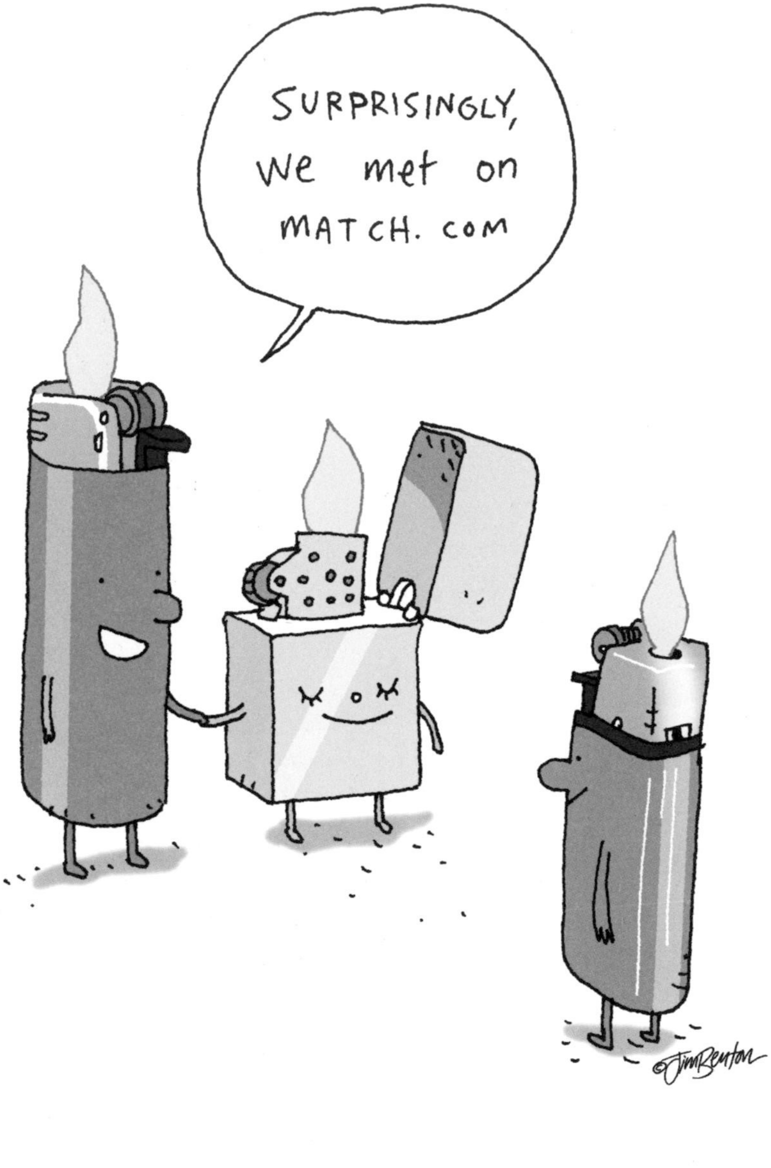
SURPRISINGLY, we met on MATCH. COM
©Jim Benton

Life is nothing but pain and sadness, misery and nameless longings.
Hey, man. I agree with you.
©Jim Benton

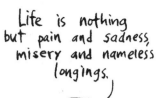

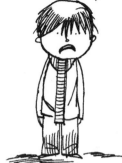

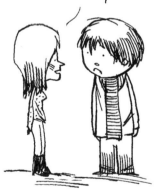

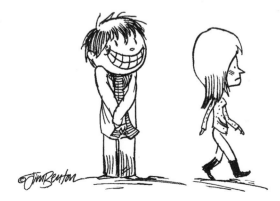

IT'S MAGIC

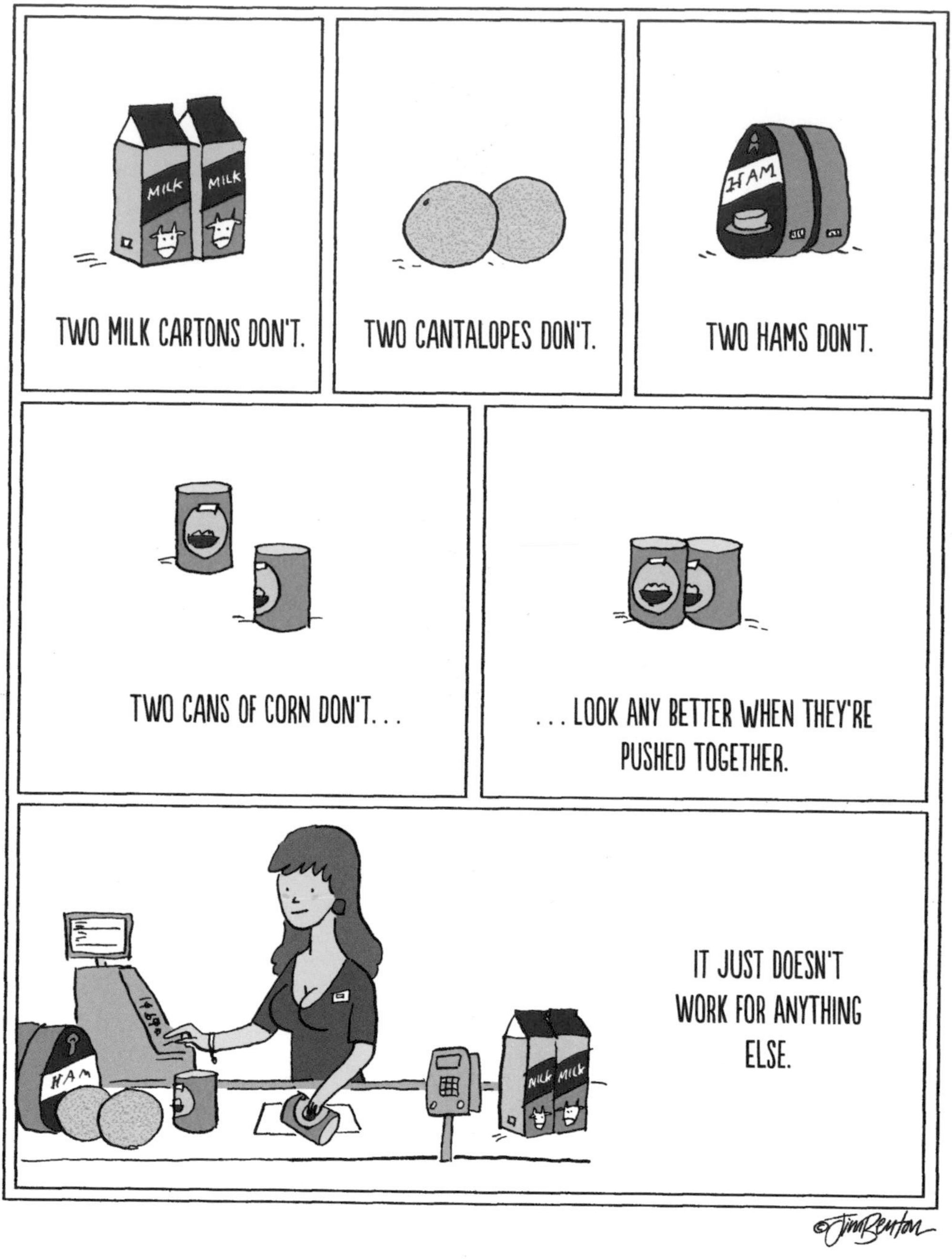
MILK
MILK
HAM
TWO MILK CARTONS DON'T.
TWO CANTALOPES DON'T.
TWO HAMS DON'T.
TWO CANS OF CORN DON'T...
...LOOK ANY BETTER WHEN THEY'RE PUSHED TOGETHER.
HAM
MILK MILK
IT JUST DOESN'T WORK FOR ANYTHING ELSE.
©Jim Benton

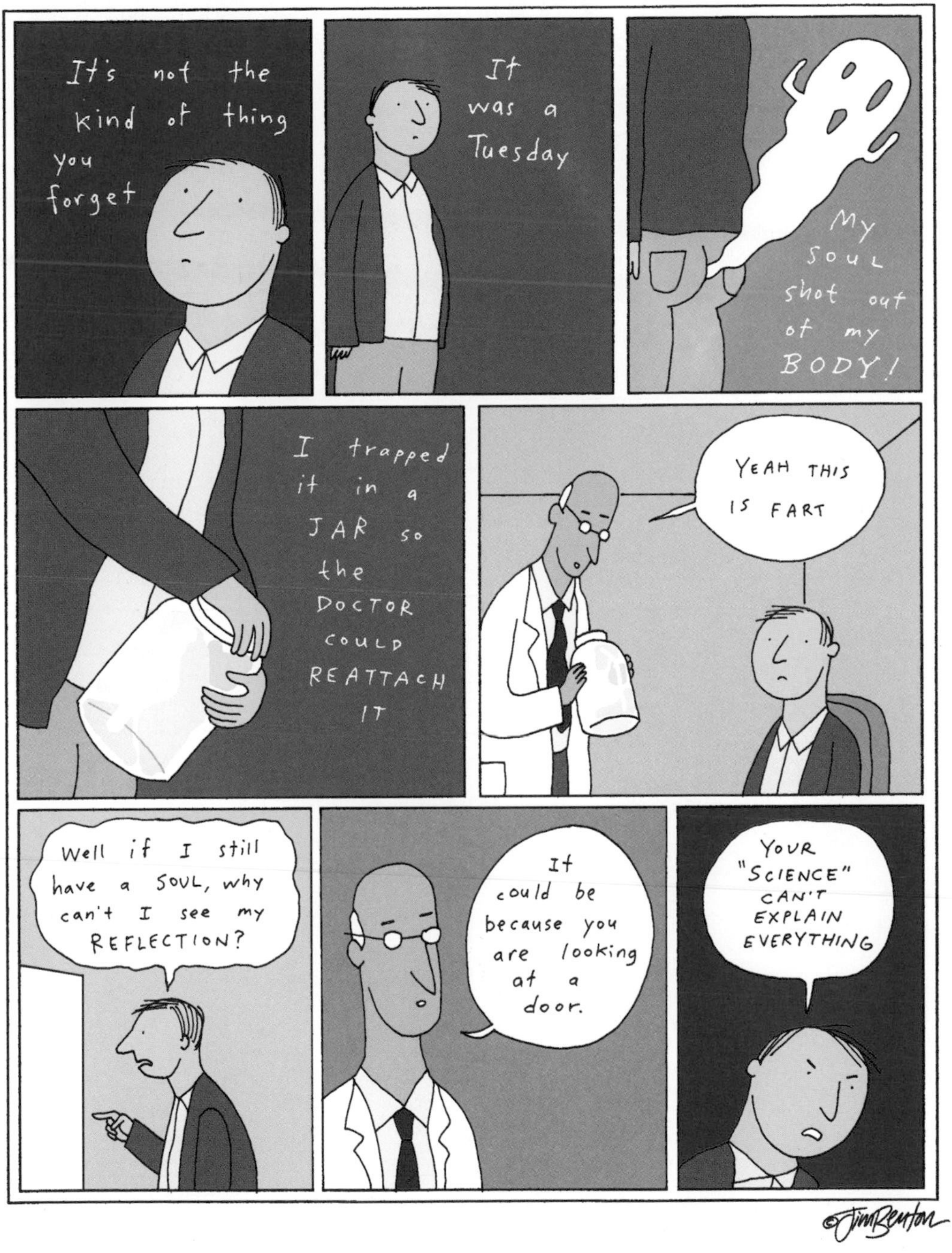
It's not the kind of thing you forget
It was a Tuesday
My soul shot out of my BODY!
I trapped it in a JAR so the DOCTOR COULD REATTACH IT
YEAH THIS IS FART
Well if I still have a SOUL, why can't I see my REFLECTION?
It could be because you are looking at a door.
YOUR "SCIENCE" CAN'T EXPLAIN EVERYTHING
©Jim Benton

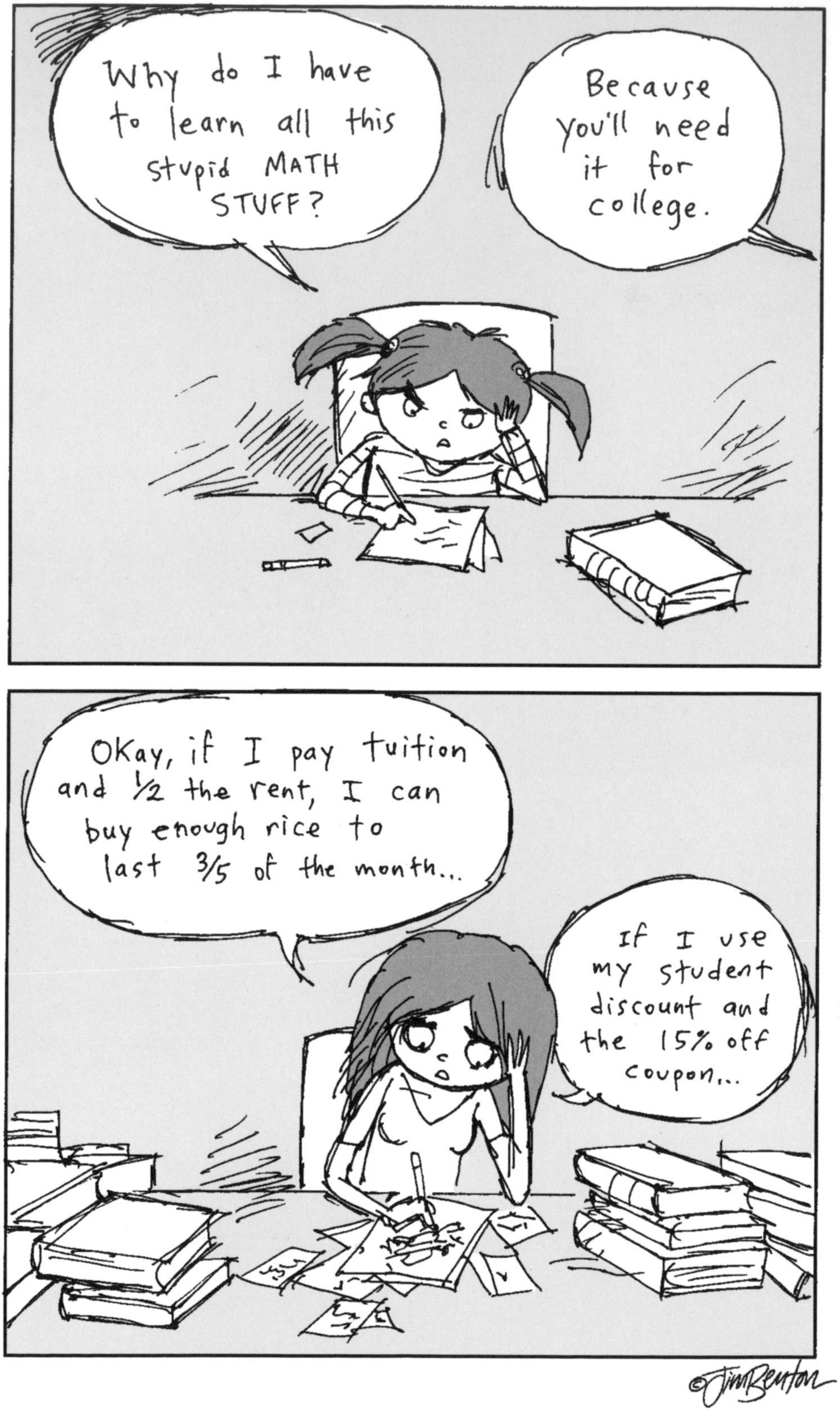
Why do I have to learn all this stupid MATH STUFF?
Because you'll need it for college.
OKay, if I pay tuition and ½ the rent, I can buy enough rice to last 3/5 of the month...
If I use my student discount and the 15% off coupon...
©Jim Benton

My Beard

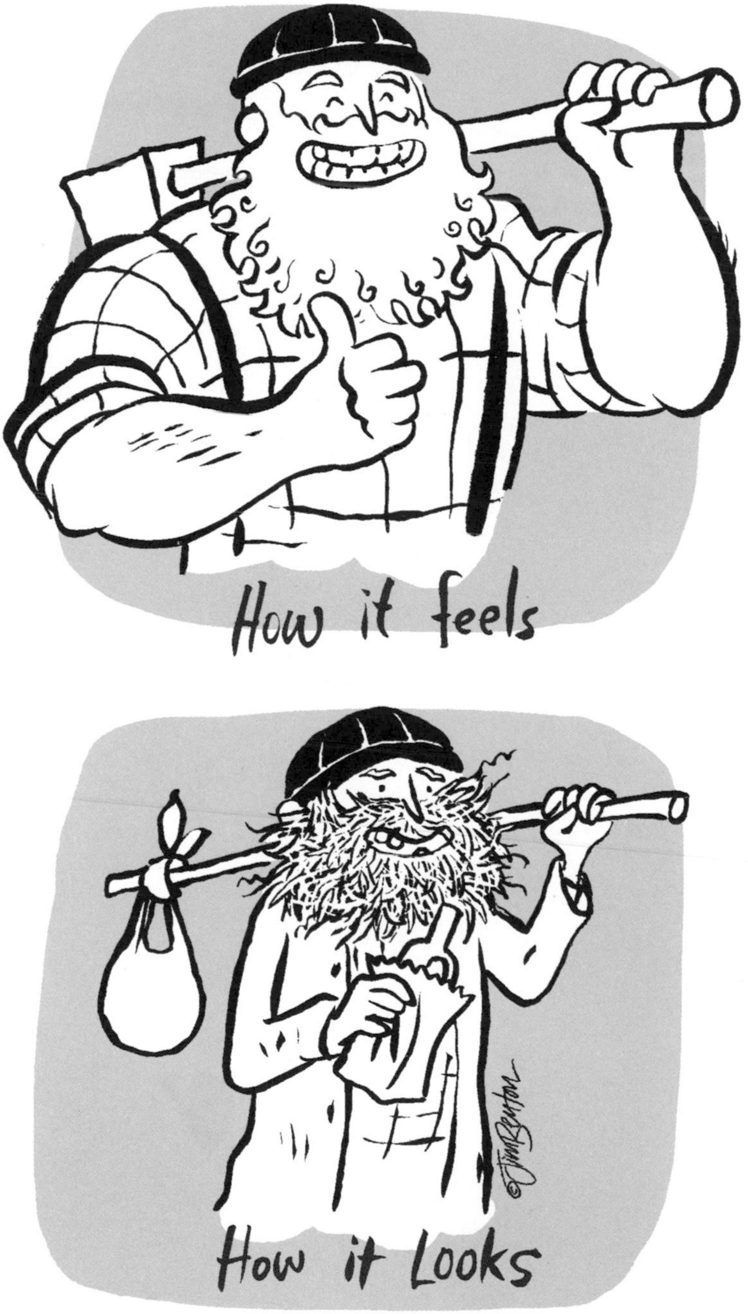
How it feels
How it Looks

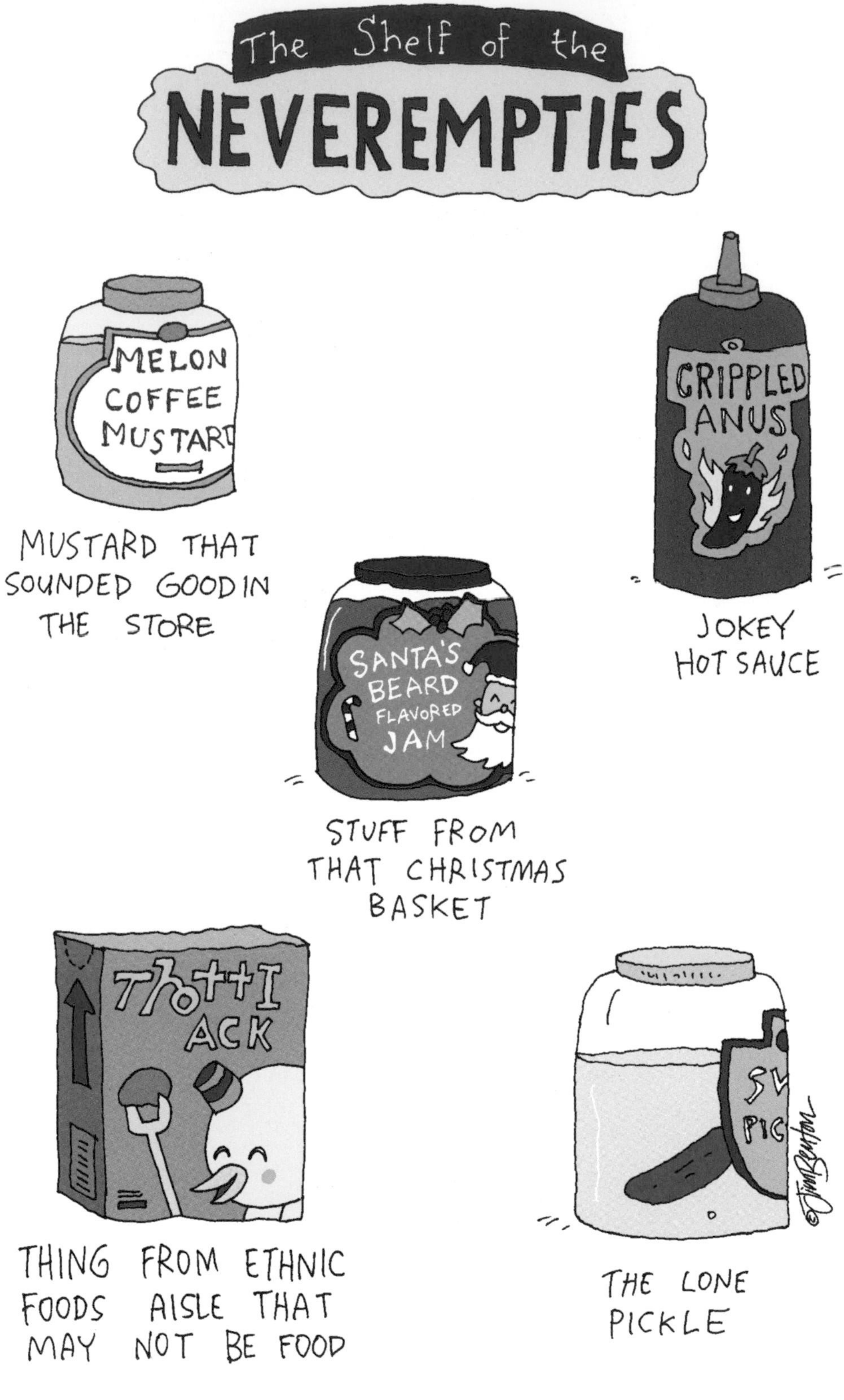
The Shelf of the
NEVEREMPTIES
MELON COFFEE MUSTARD
MUSTARD THAT SOUNDED GOOD IN THE STORE
CRIPPLED ANUS
JOKEY HOT SAUCE
SANTA'S BEARD FLAVORED JAM
STUFF FROM THAT CHRISTMAS BASKET
ACK
THING FROM ETHNIC FOODS AISLE THAT MAY NOT BE FOOD
THE LONE PICKLE
©Jim Benton

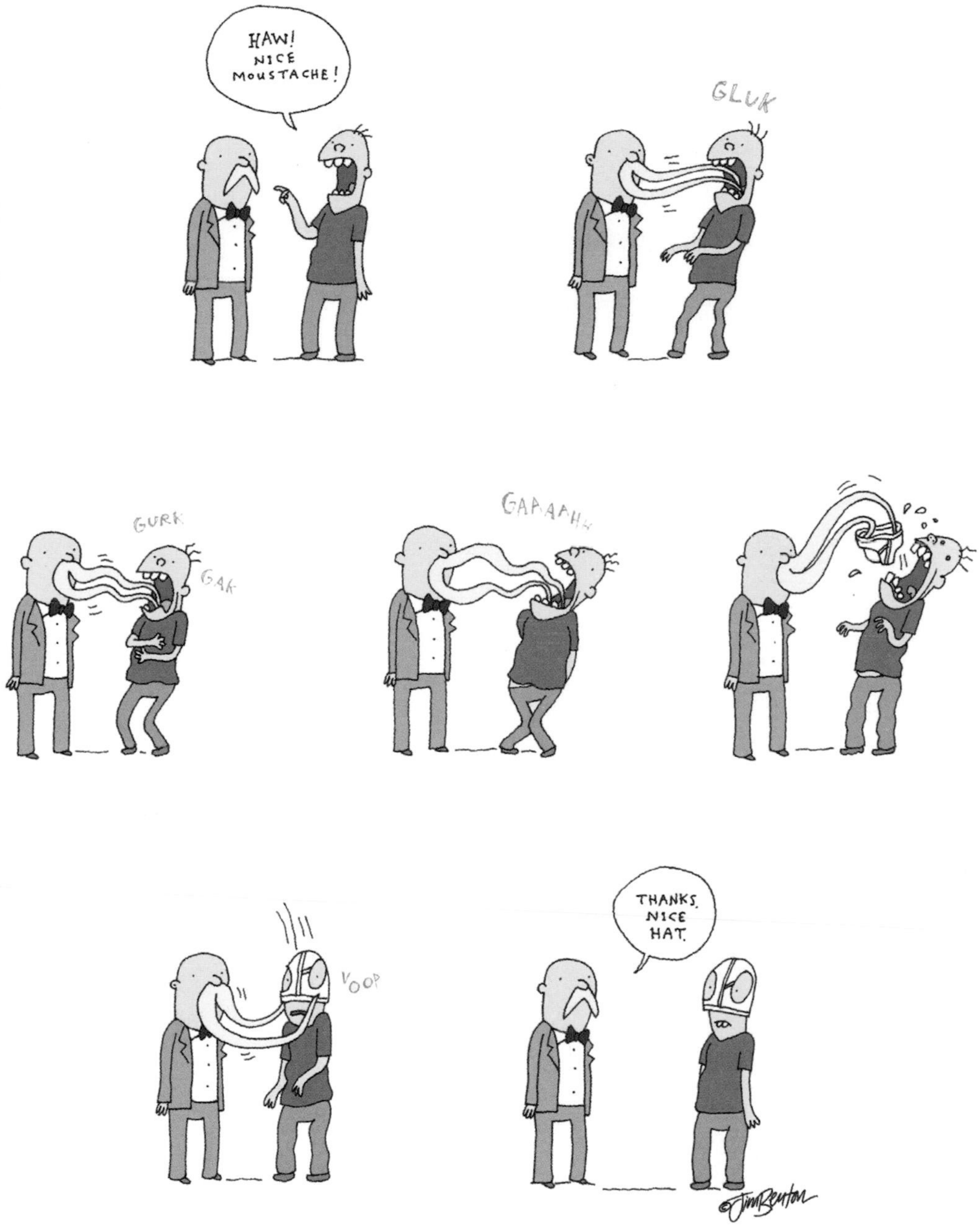
HAW! NICE MOUSTACHE!
GLUK
GURK
GAK
GAAAAHH
VOOP
THANKS. NICE HAT.
©Jim Benton

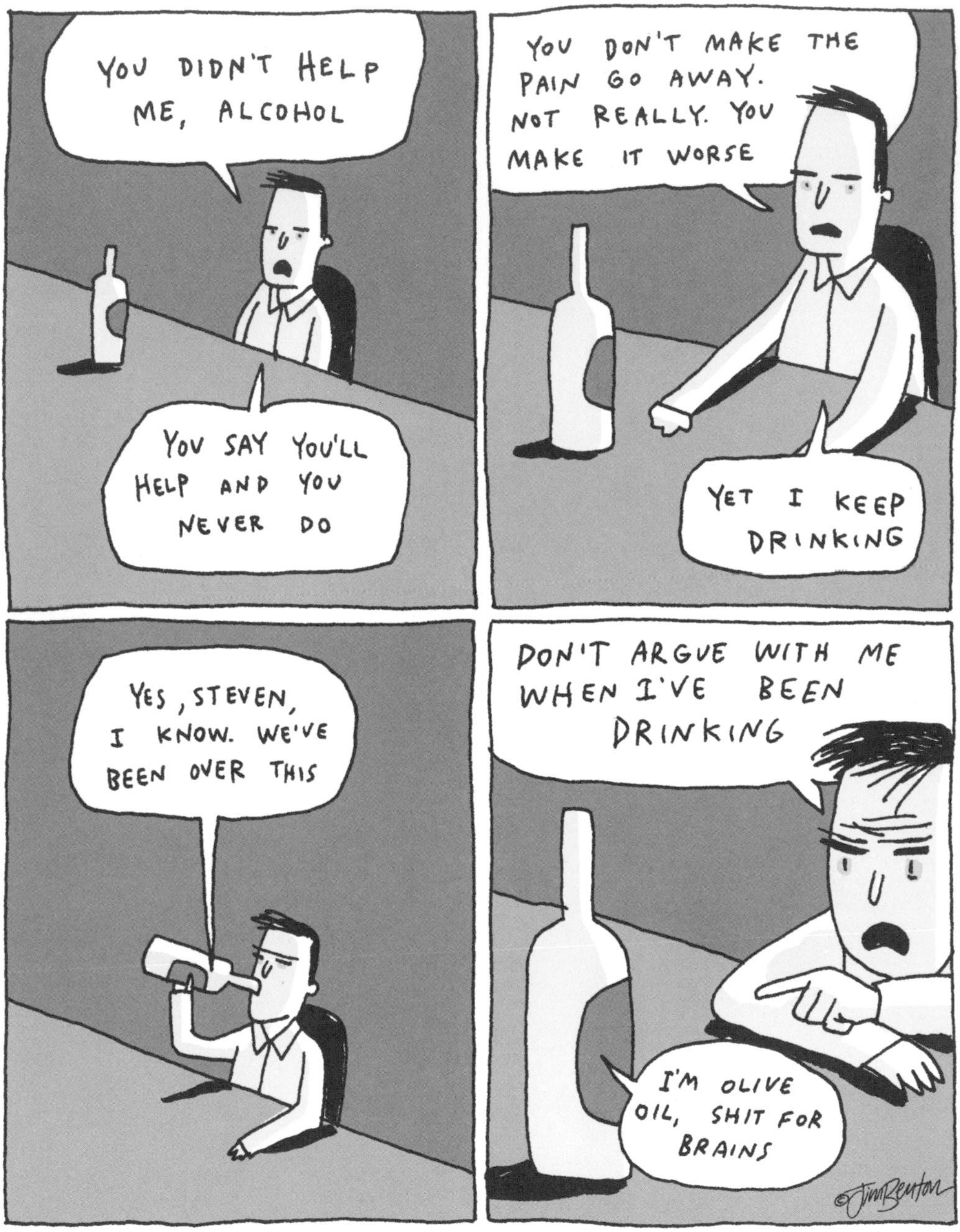
YOU DIDN'T HELP ME, ALCOHOL
YOU SAY YOU'LL HELP AND YOU NEVER DO
YOU DON'T MAKE THE PAIN GO AWAY. NOT REALLY. YOU MAKE IT WORSE
YET I KEEP DRINKING
YES, STEVEN, I KNOW. WE'VE BEEN OVER THIS
DON'T ARGUE WITH ME WHEN I'VE BEEN DRINKING
I'M OLIVE OIL, SHIT FOR BRAINS
©Jim Benton

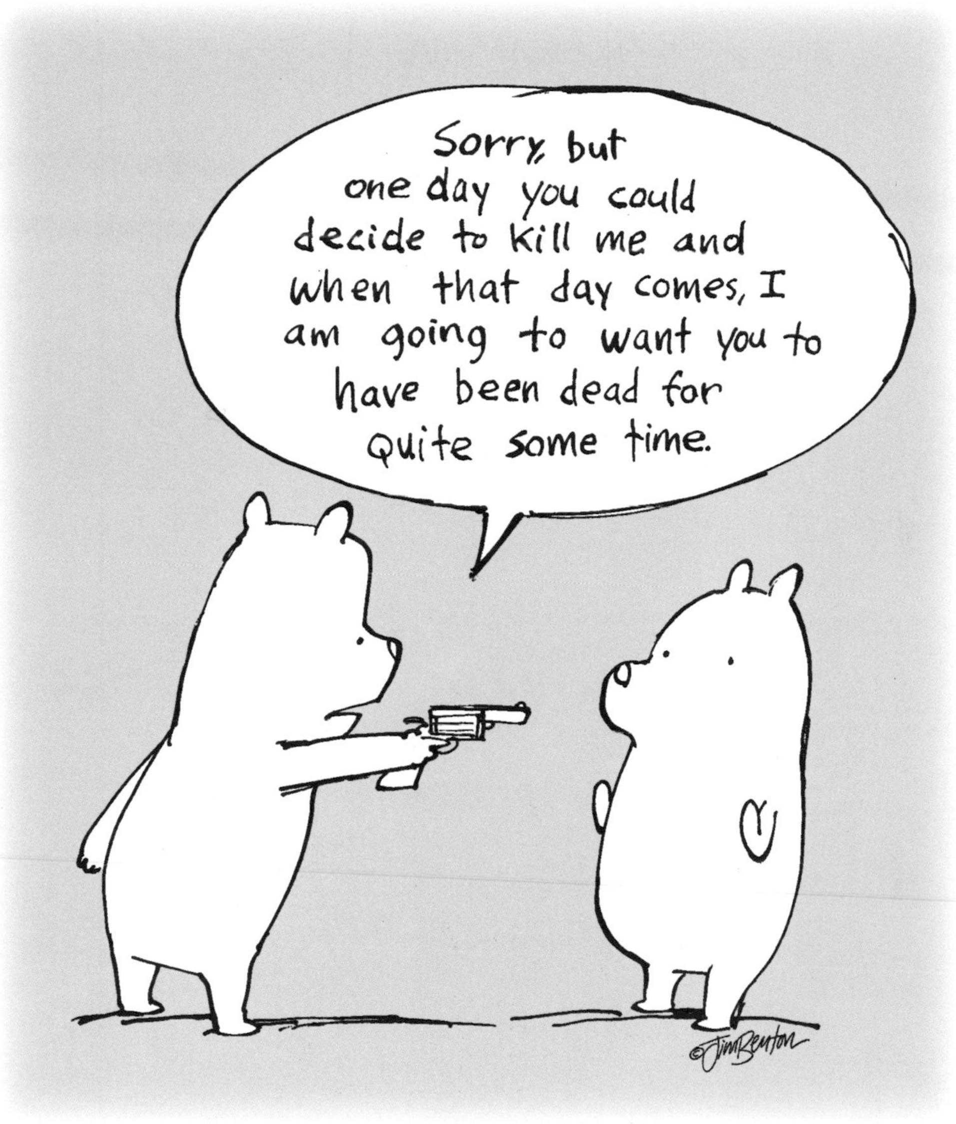
Sorry, but one day you could decide to kill me and when that day comes, I am going to want you to have been dead for quite some time.
©Jim Benton

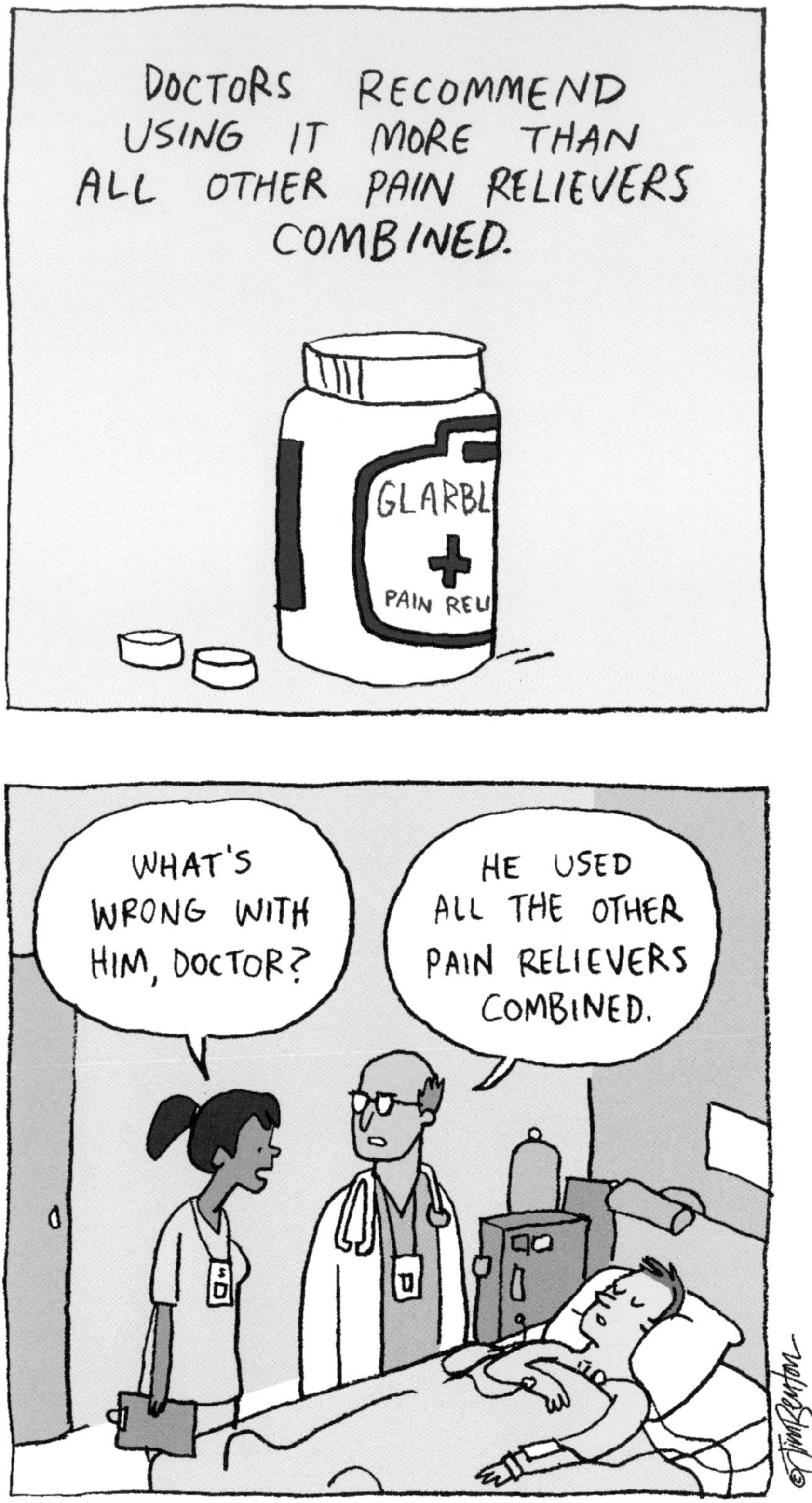
DOCTORS RECOMMEND USING IT MORE THAN ALL OTHER PAIN RELIEVERS COMBINED.
GLARBL
PAIN RELI
WHAT'S WRONG WITH HIM, DOCTOR?
HE USED ALL THE OTHER PAIN RELIEVERS COMBINED.

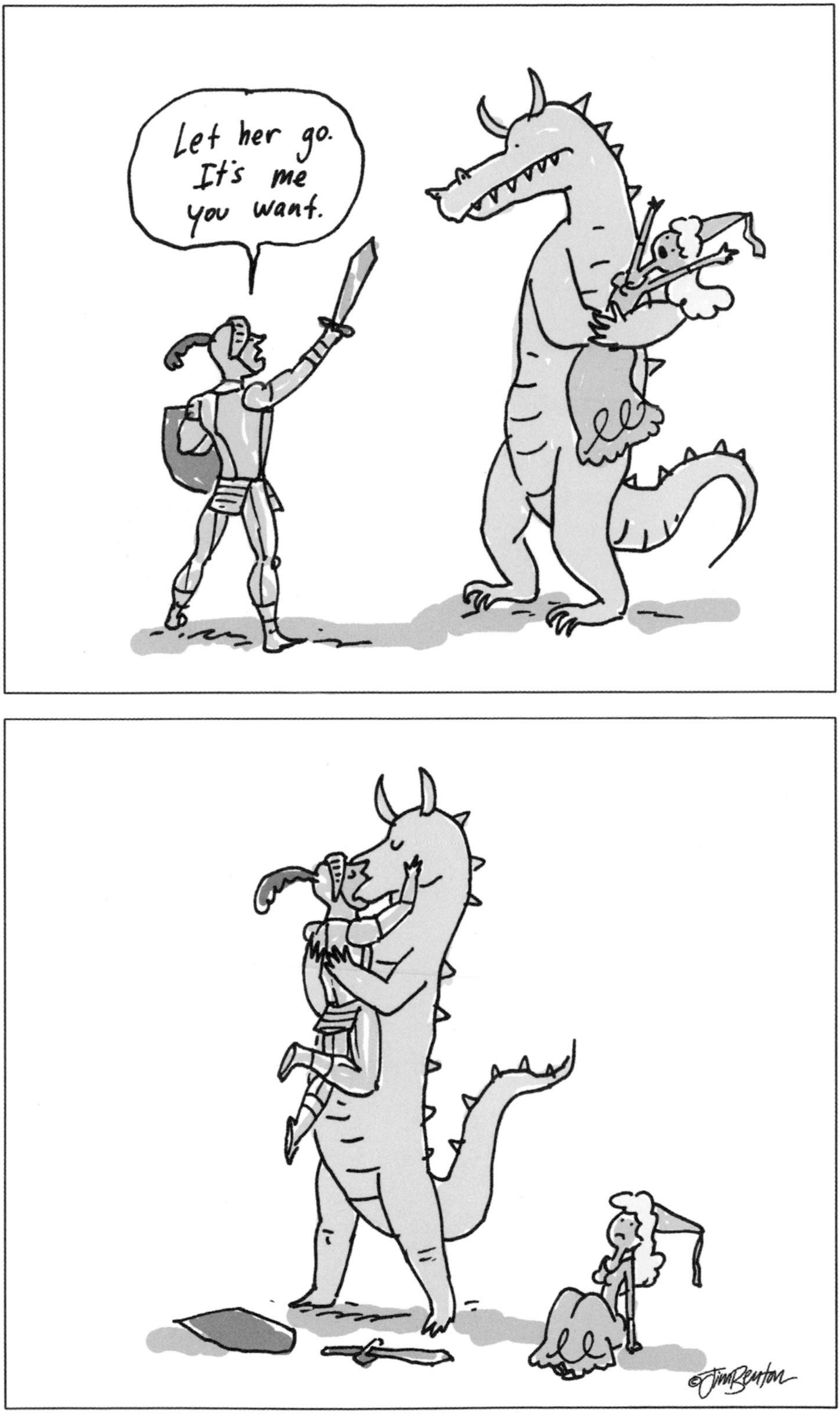
Let her go. It's me you want.
©Jim Benton

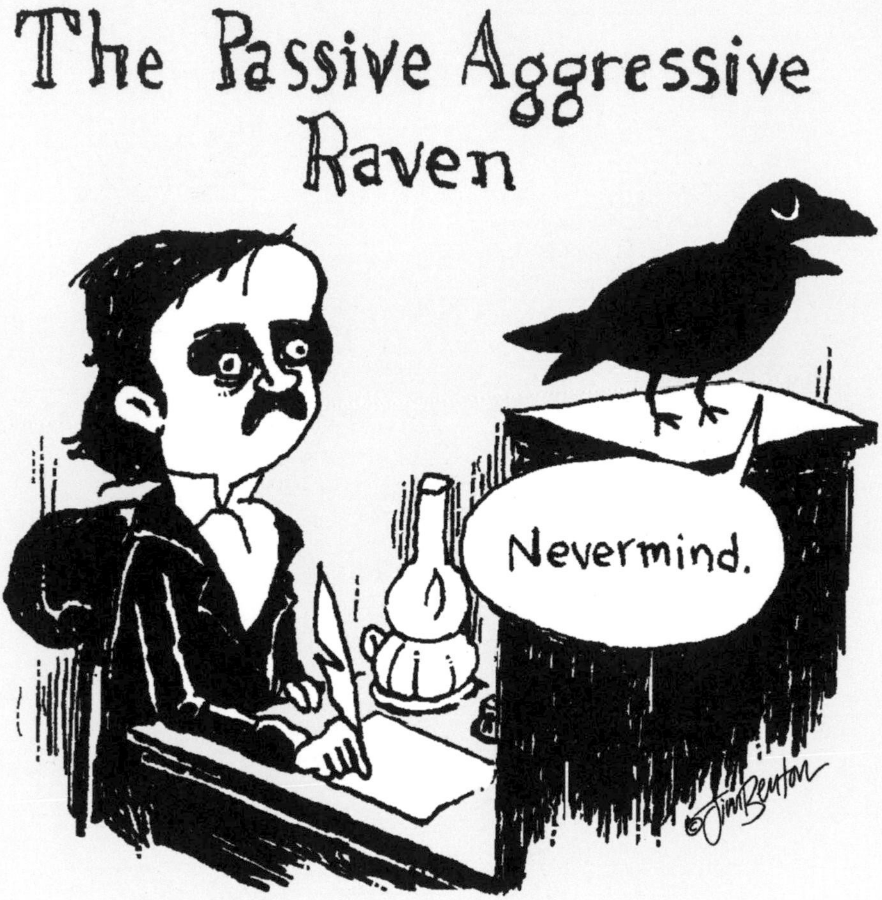
The Passive Aggressive Raven
Nevermind.
©Jim Benton

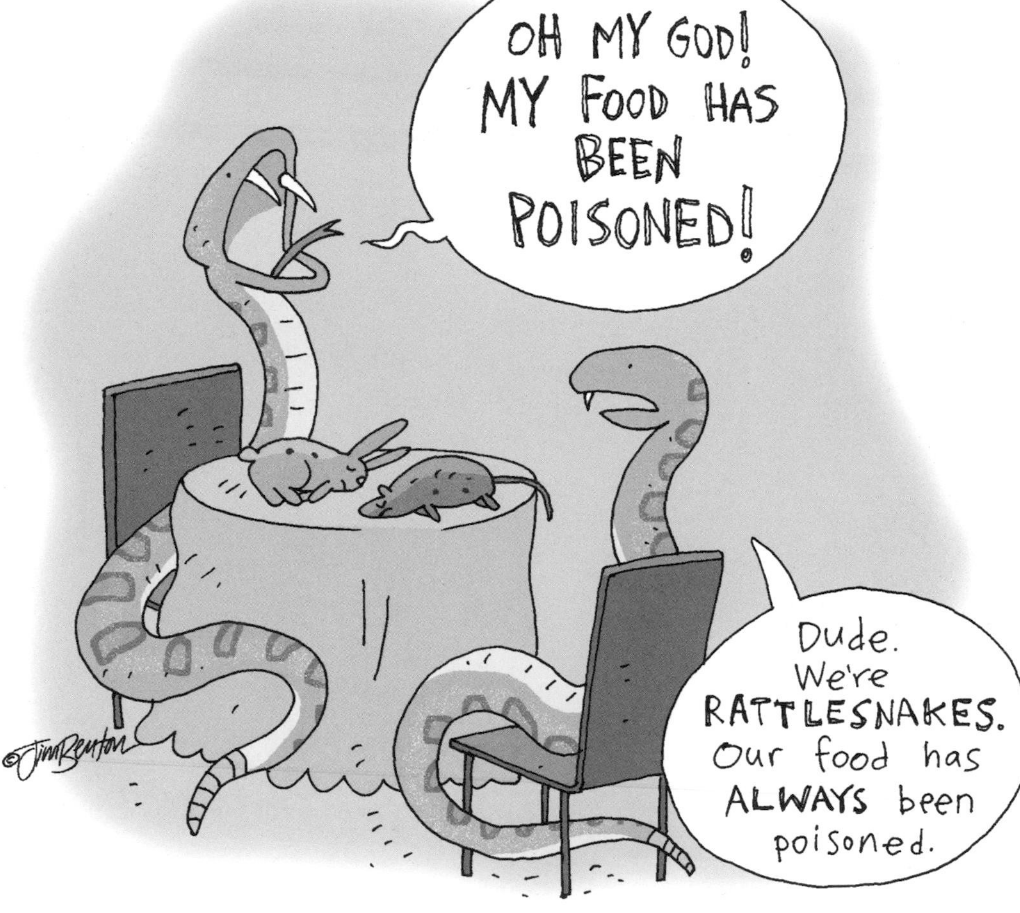
OH MY GOD! MY FOOD HAS BEEN POISONED!
Dude. We're RATTLESNAKES. Our food has ALWAYS been poisoned.
©Jim Benton

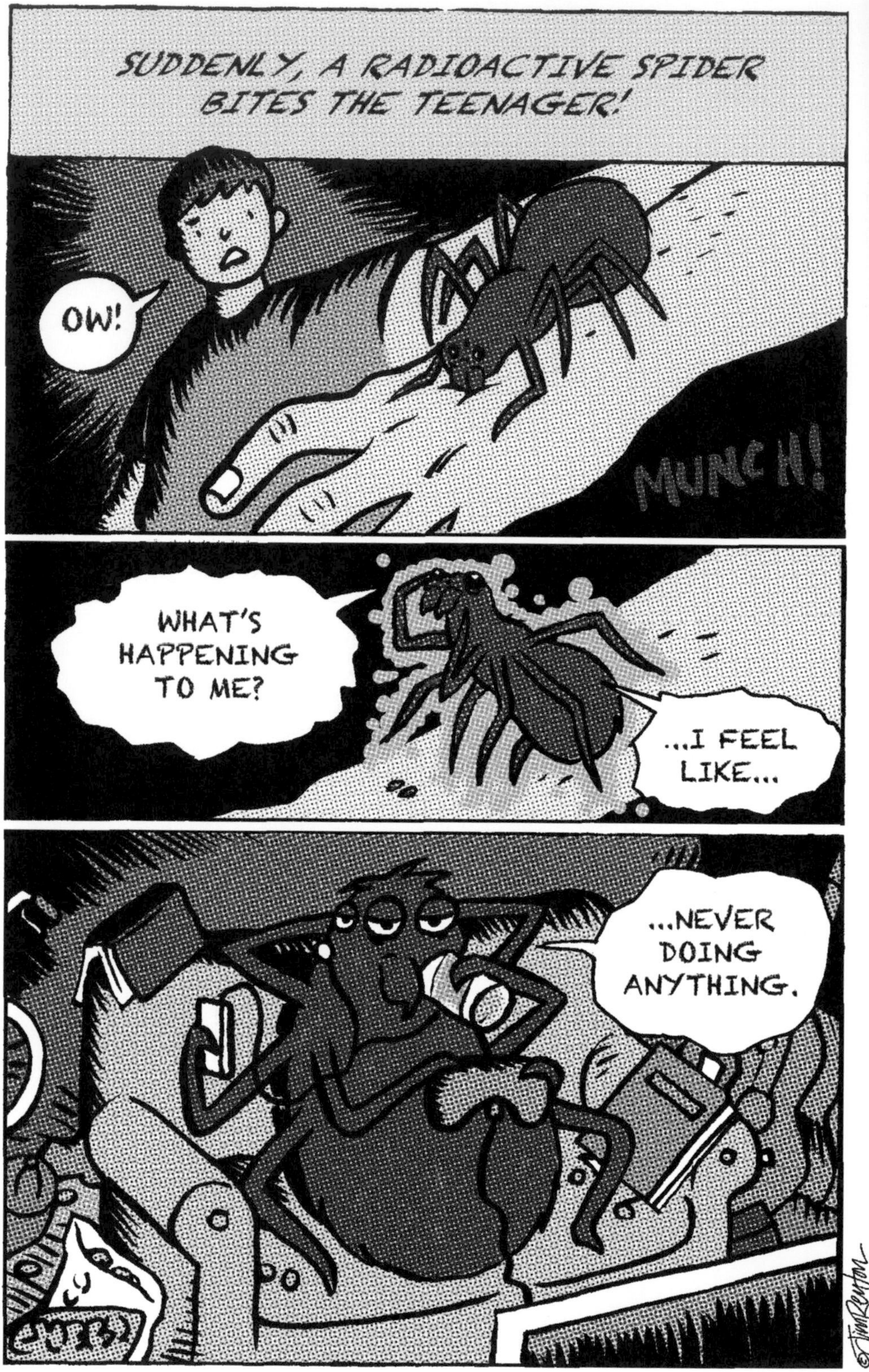
SUDDENLY, A RADIOACTIVE SPIDER BITES THE TEENAGER!
OW!
MUNCH!
WHAT'S HAPPENING TO ME?
...I FEEL LIKE...
...NEVER DOING ANYTHING.
©Jim Benton

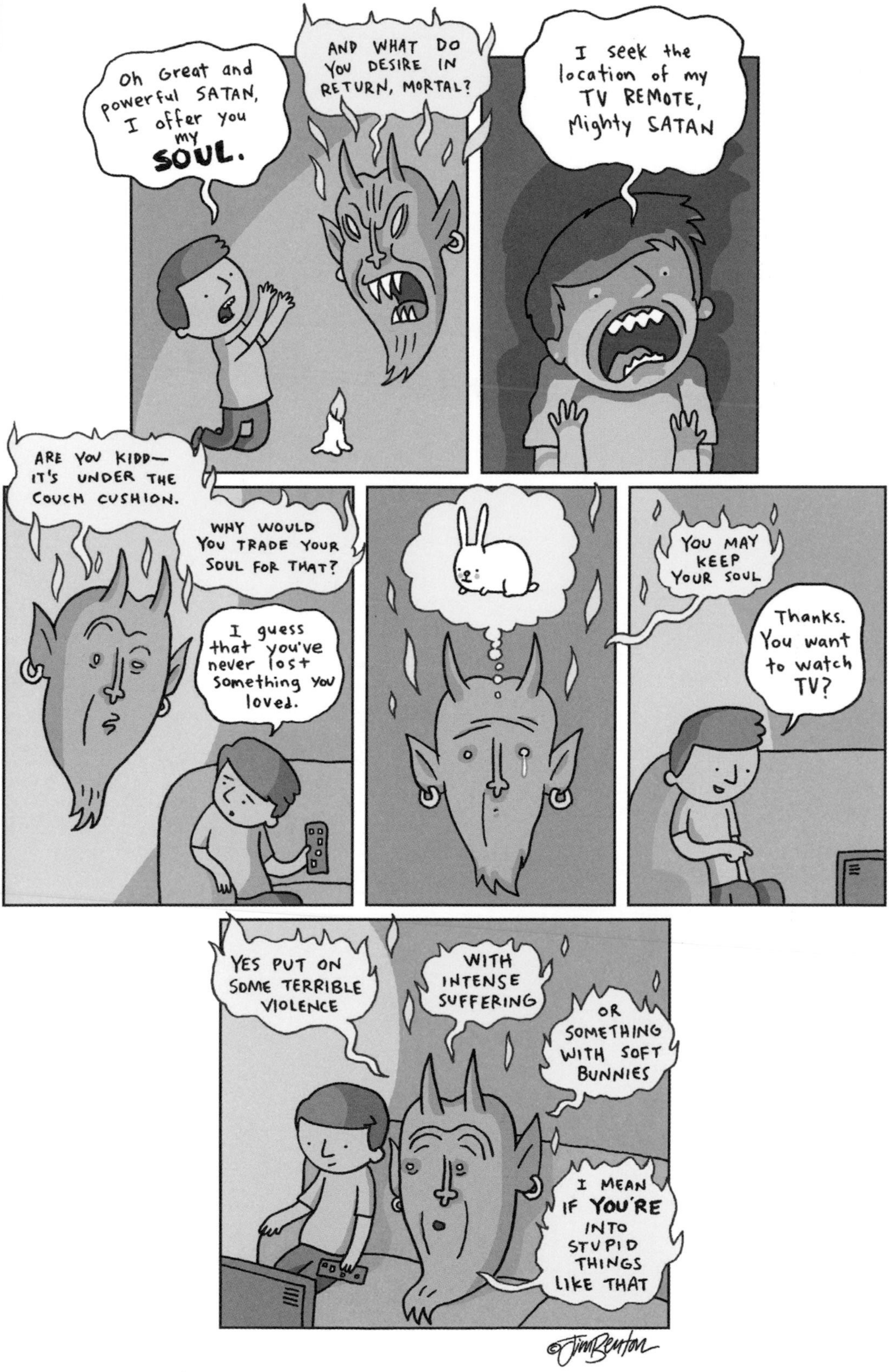
Oh Great and powerful SATAN, I offer you my SOUL.
AND WHAT DO YOU DESIRE IN RETURN, MORTAL?
I seek the location of my TV REMOTE, Mighty SATAN
ARE YOU KIDD— IT'S UNDER THE COUCH CUSHION.
WHY WOULD YOU TRADE YOUR SOUL FOR THAT?
I guess that you've never lost something you loved.
YOU MAY KEEP YOUR SOUL
Thanks. You want to watch TV?
YES PUT ON SOME TERRIBLE VIOLENCE
WITH INTENSE SUFFERING
OR SOMETHING WITH SOFT BUNNIES
I MEAN IF YOU'RE INTO STUPID THINGS LIKE THAT
©Jim Benton

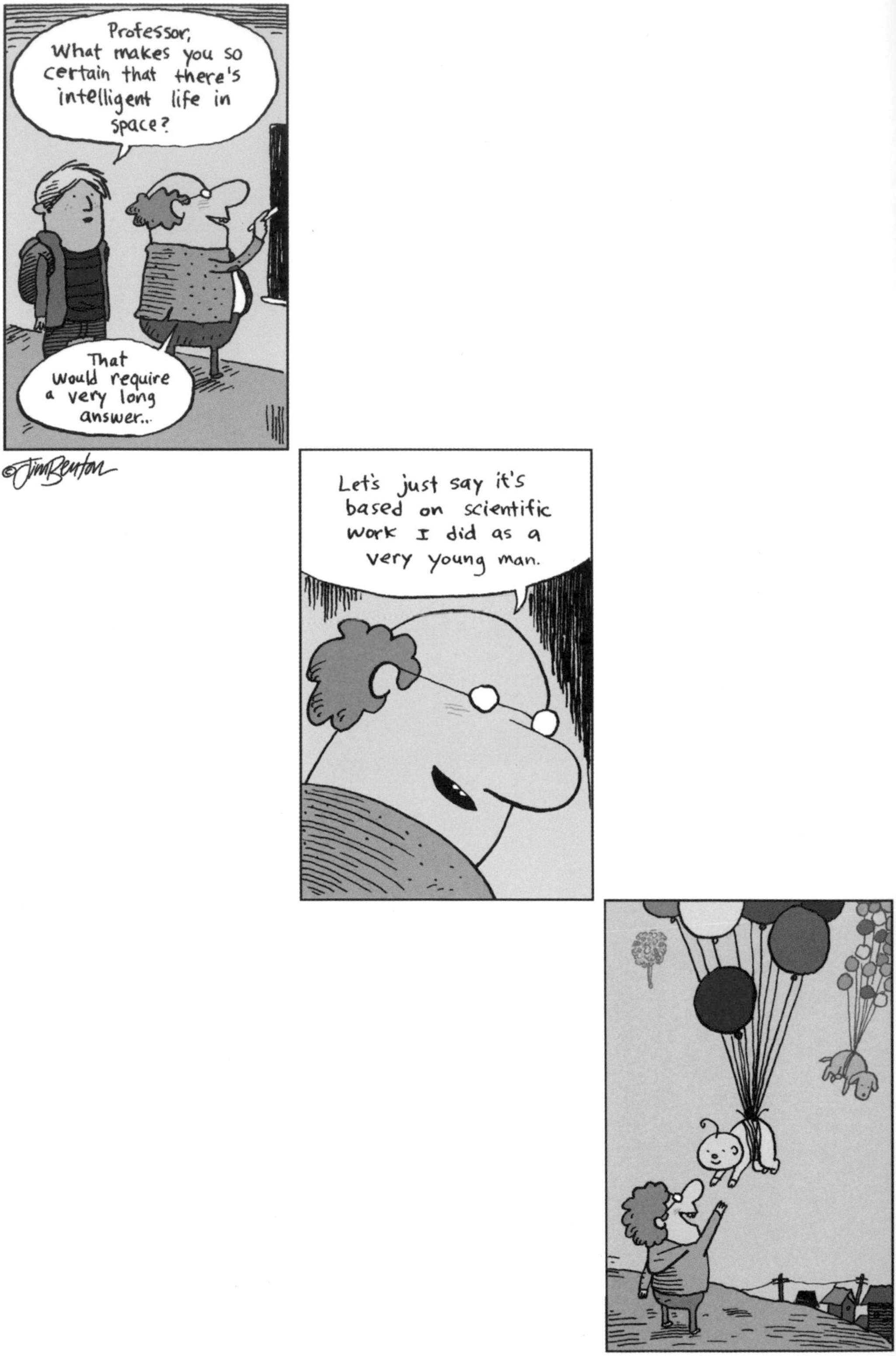
Professor, What makes you so certain that there's intelligent life in space?
That would require a very long answer..
©JimBenton
Let's just say it's based on scientific work I did as a very young man.

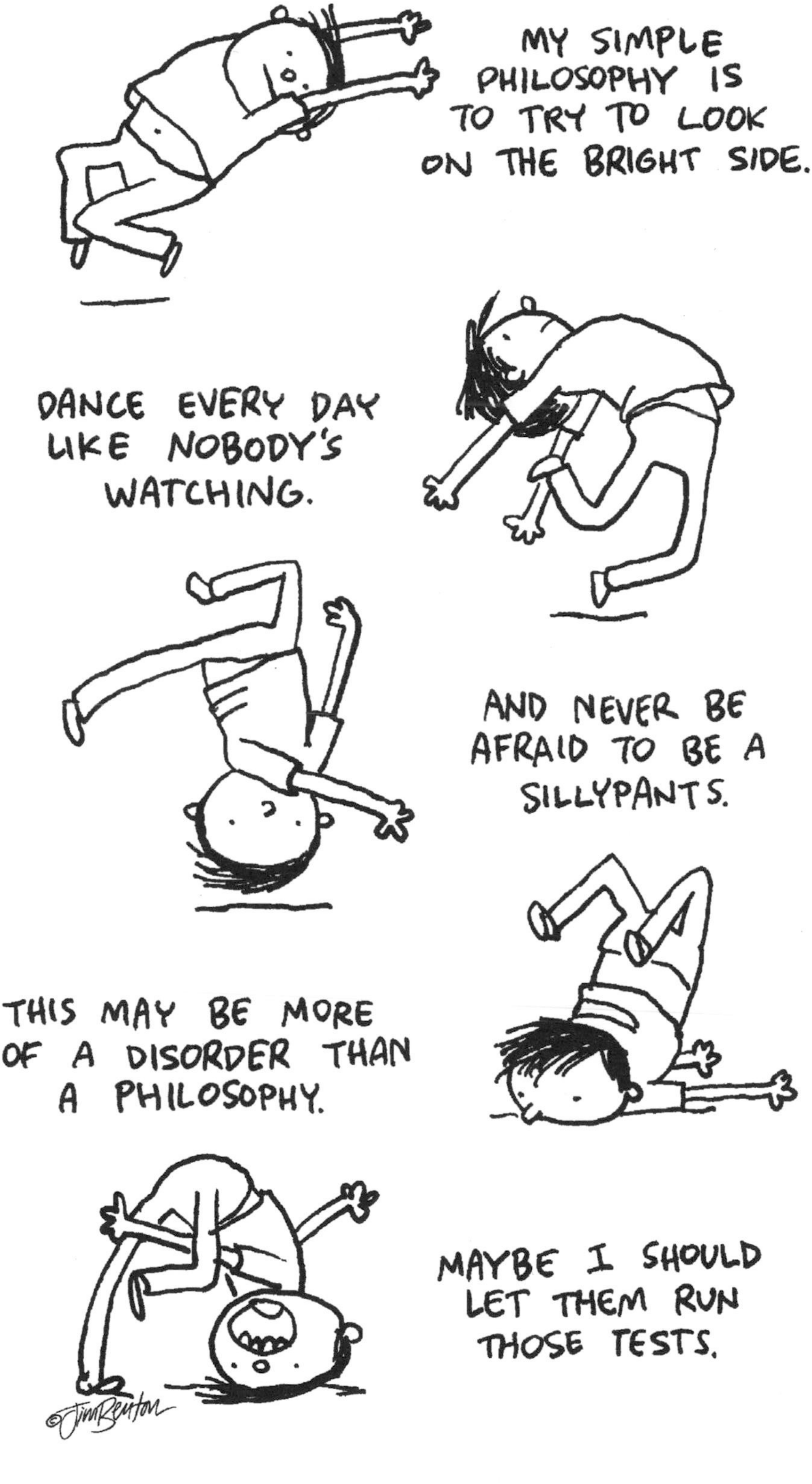
MY SIMPLE PHILOSOPHY IS TO TRY TO LOOK ON THE BRIGHT SIDE.
DANCE EVERY DAY LIKE NOBODY'S WATCHING.
AND NEVER BE AFRAID TO BE A SILLYPANTS.
THIS MAY BE MORE OF A DISORDER THAN A PHILOSOPHY.
MAYBE I SHOULD LET THEM RUN THOSE TESTS.
©Jim Benton

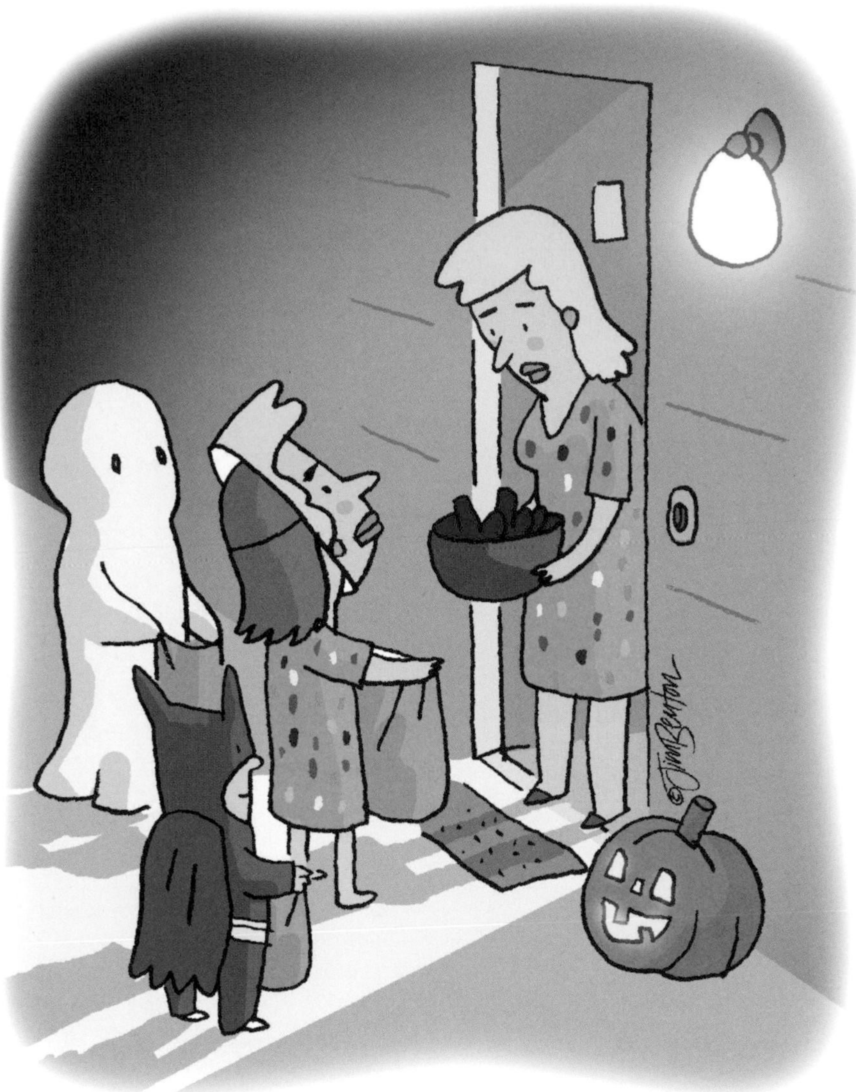
©Jim Benton

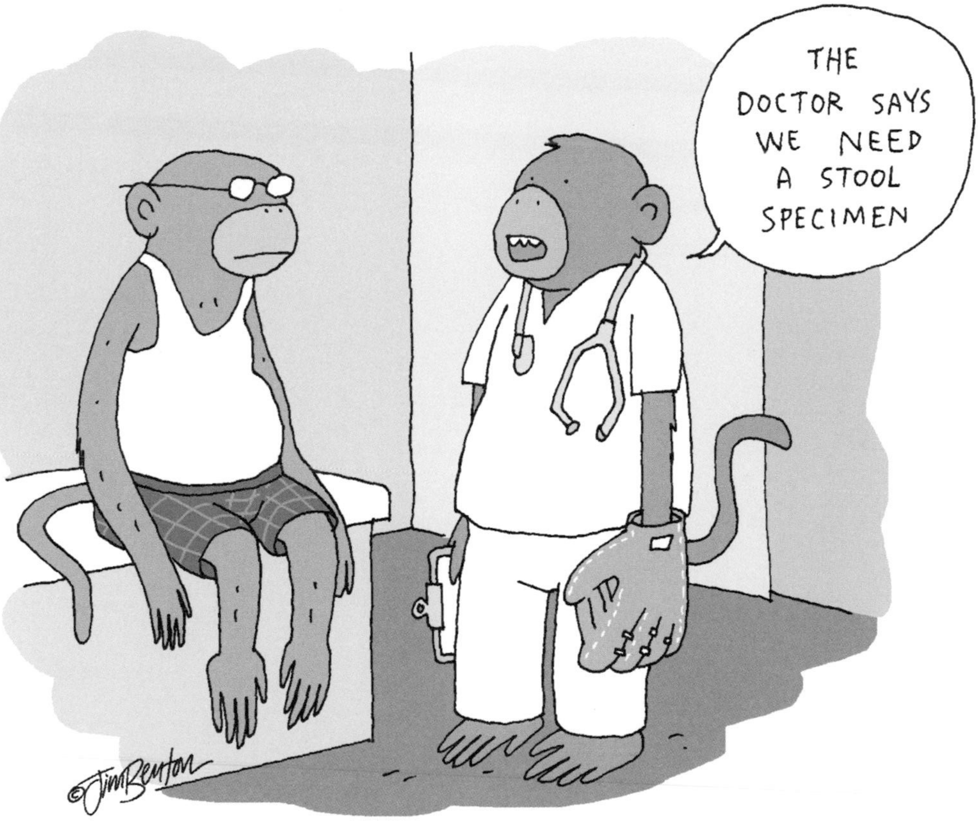
THE DOCTOR SAYS WE NEED A STOOL SPECIMEN
©Jim Benton

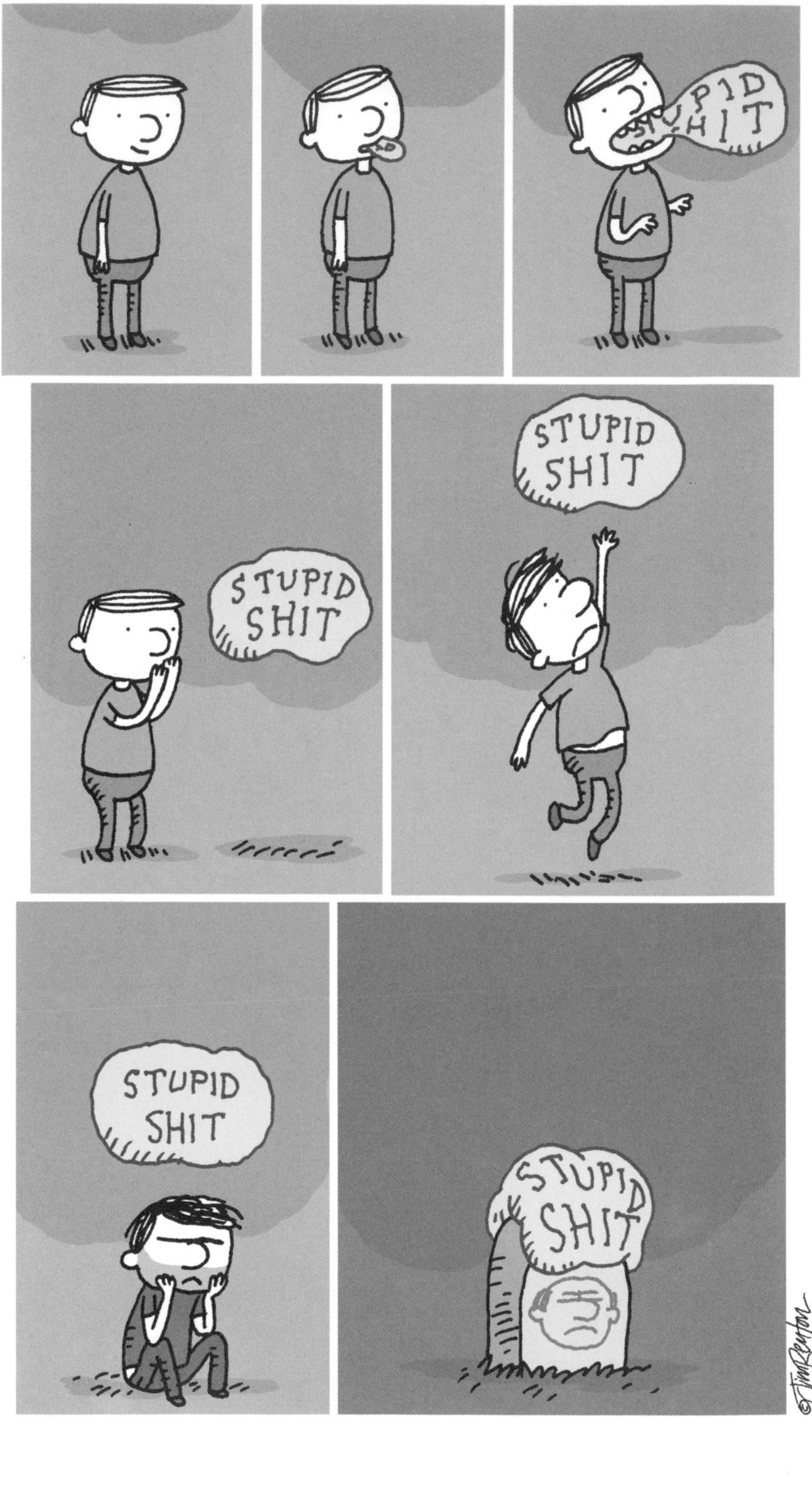
STUPID SHIT
STUPID SHIT
STUPID SHIT
STUPID SHIT

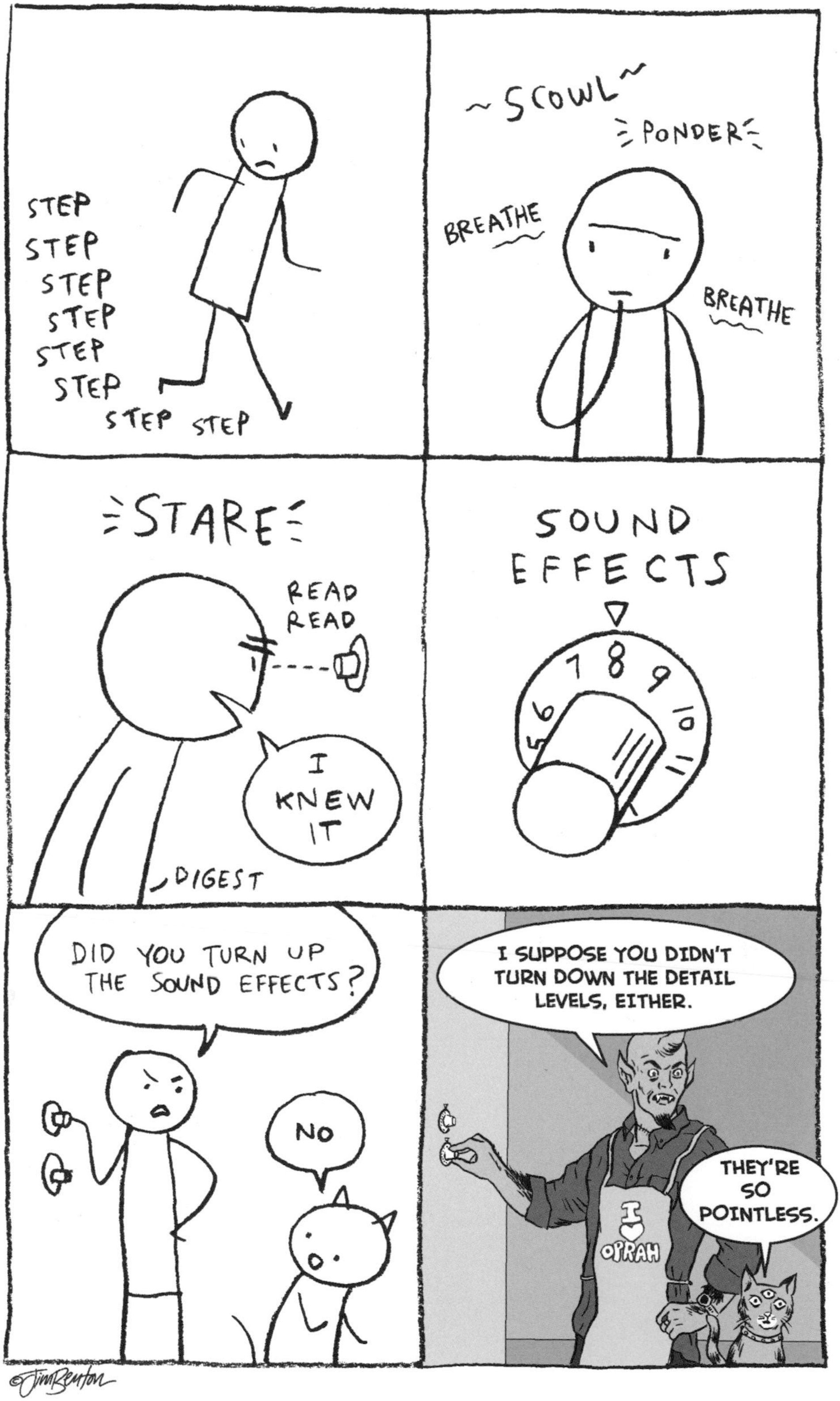
STEP
STEP
STEP
STEP
STEP
STEP
STEP STEP
~SCOWL~
PONDER
BREATHE
BREATHE
STARE
READ
READ
I KNEW IT
DIGEST
SOUND EFFECTS
7 8 9
5 6
10
11
DID YOU TURN UP THE SOUND EFFECTS?
NO
I SUPPOSE YOU DIDN'T TURN DOWN THE DETAIL LEVELS, EITHER.
I ♥ OPRAH
THEY'RE SO POINTLESS.
©Jim Benton

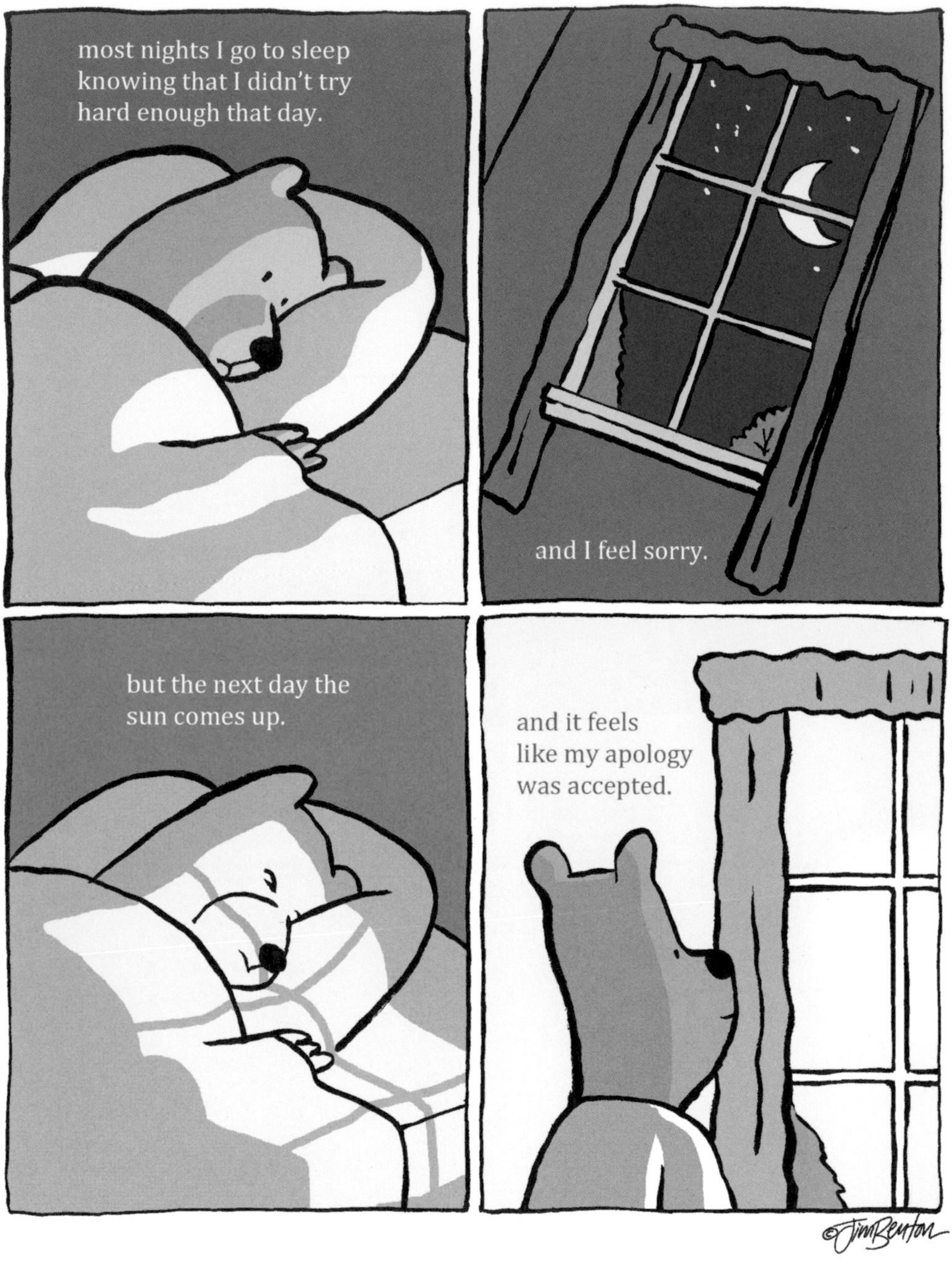
most nights I go to sleep knowing that I didn't try hard enough that day.
and I feel sorry.
but the next day the sun comes up.
and it feels like my apology was accepted.
©JimBenton

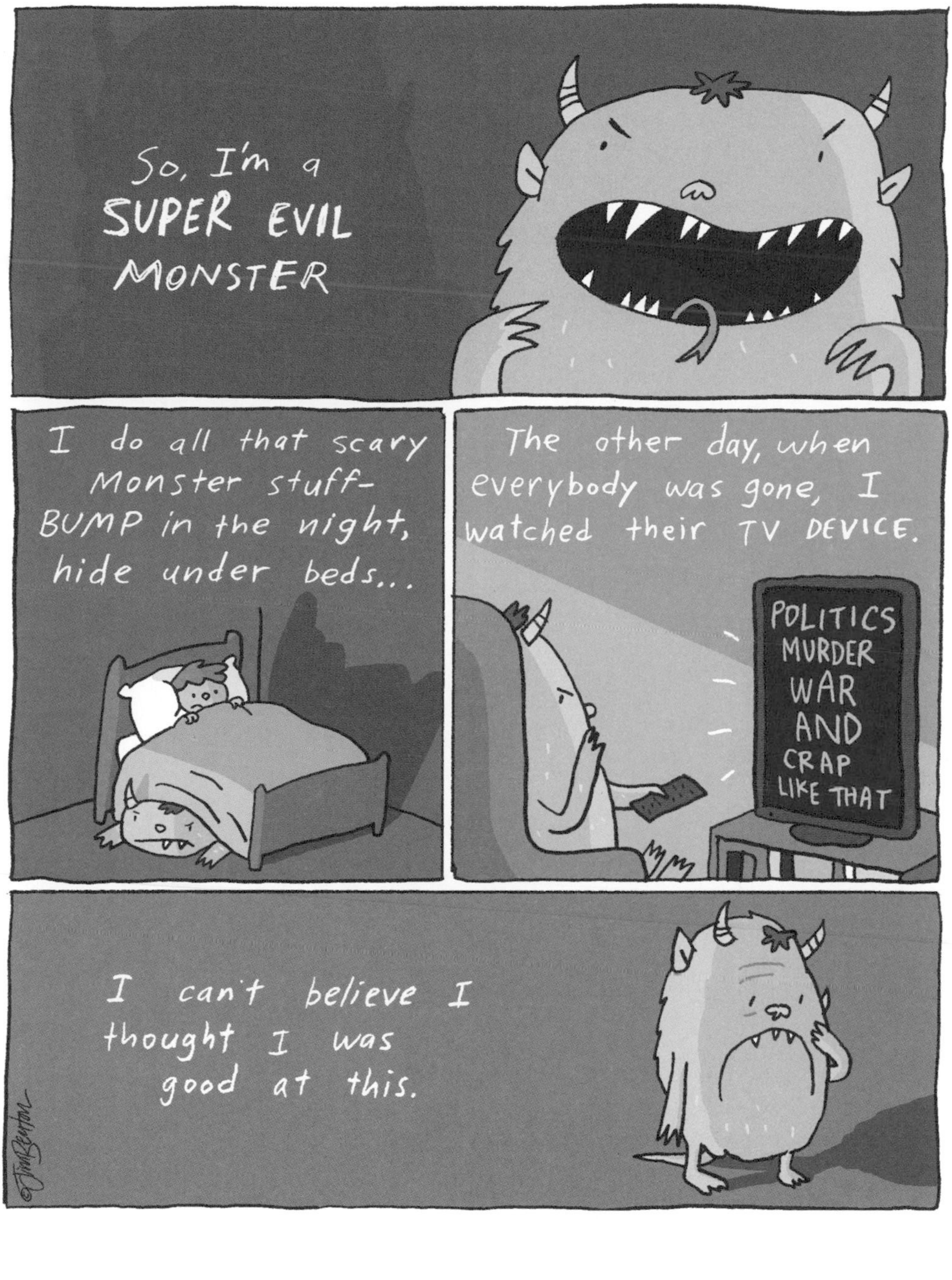
So, I'm a SUPER EVIL MONSTER
I do all that scary monster stuff- BUMP in the night, hide under beds...
The other day, when everybody was gone, I watched their TV DEVICE.
POLITICS MURDER WAR AND CRAP LIKE THAT
I can't believe I thought I was good at this.

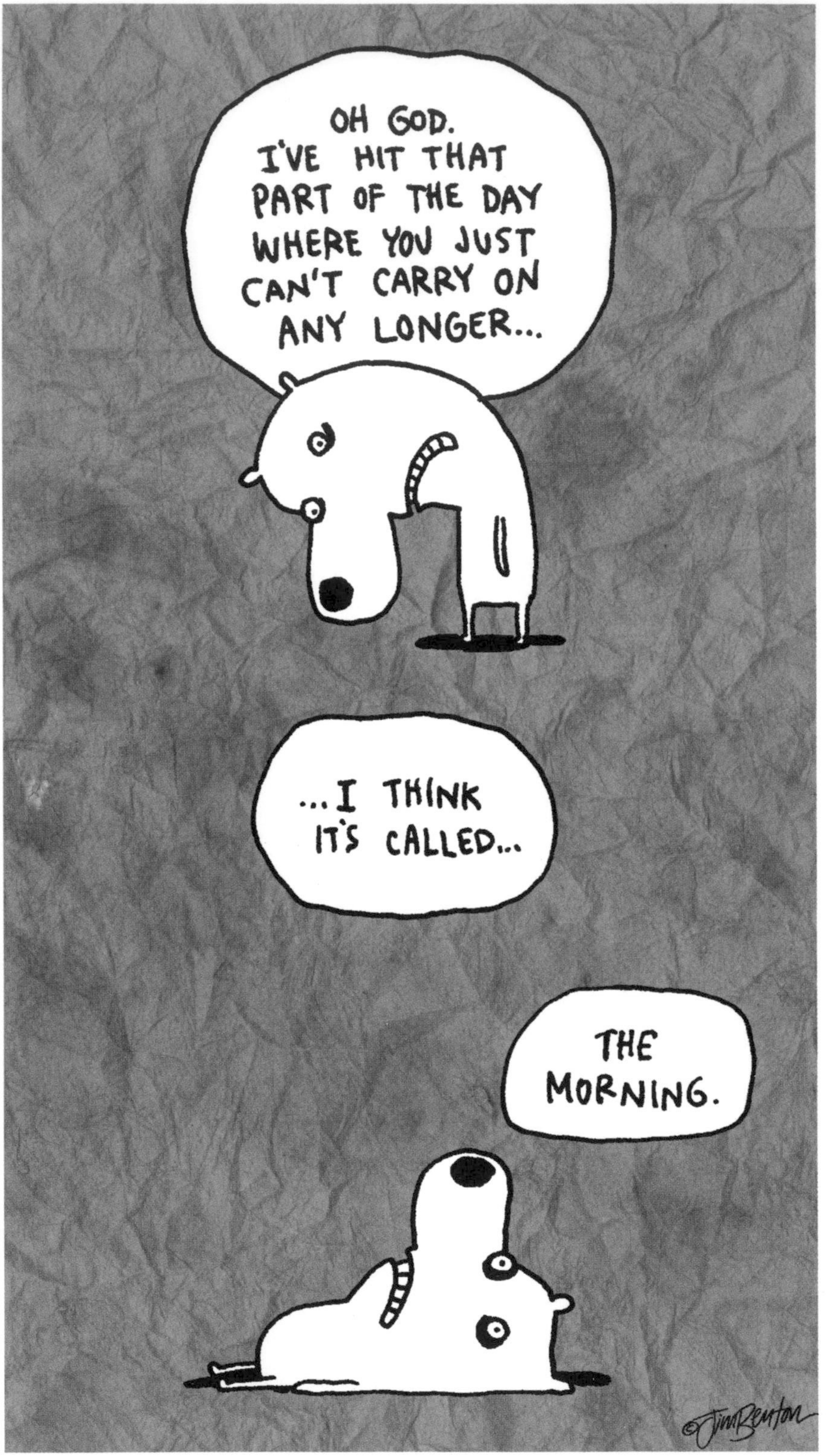
OH GOD. I'VE HIT THAT PART OF THE DAY WHERE YOU JUST CAN'T CARRY ON ANY LONGER...
...I THINK IT'S CALLED...
THE MORNING.
©Jim Benton

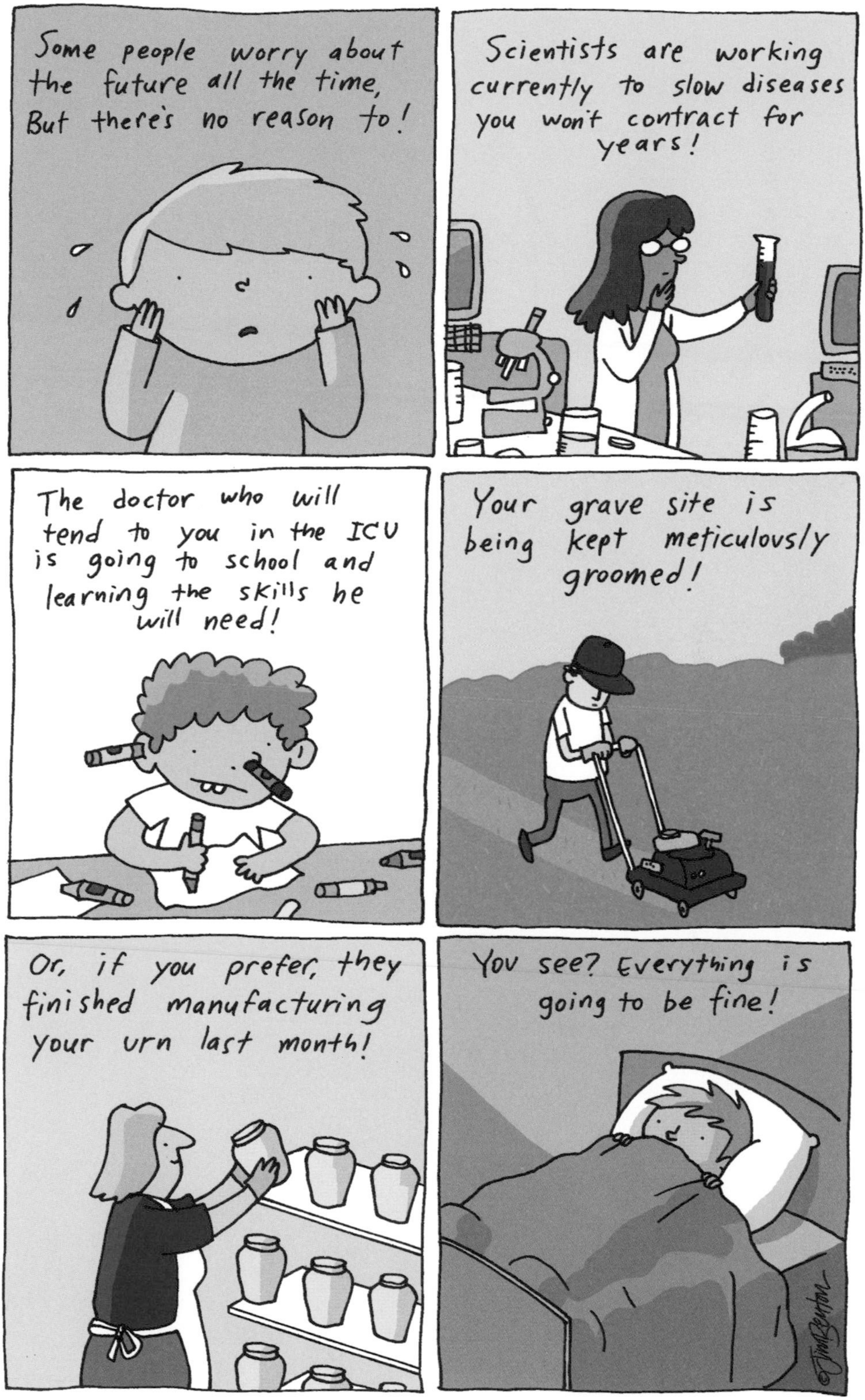
Some people worry about the future all the time, But there's no reason to!
Scientists are working currently to slow diseases you won't contract for years!
The doctor who will tend to you in the ICU is going to school and learning the skills he will need!
Your grave site is being kept meticulously groomed!
Or, if you prefer, they finished manufacturing your urn last month!
You see? Everything is going to be fine!

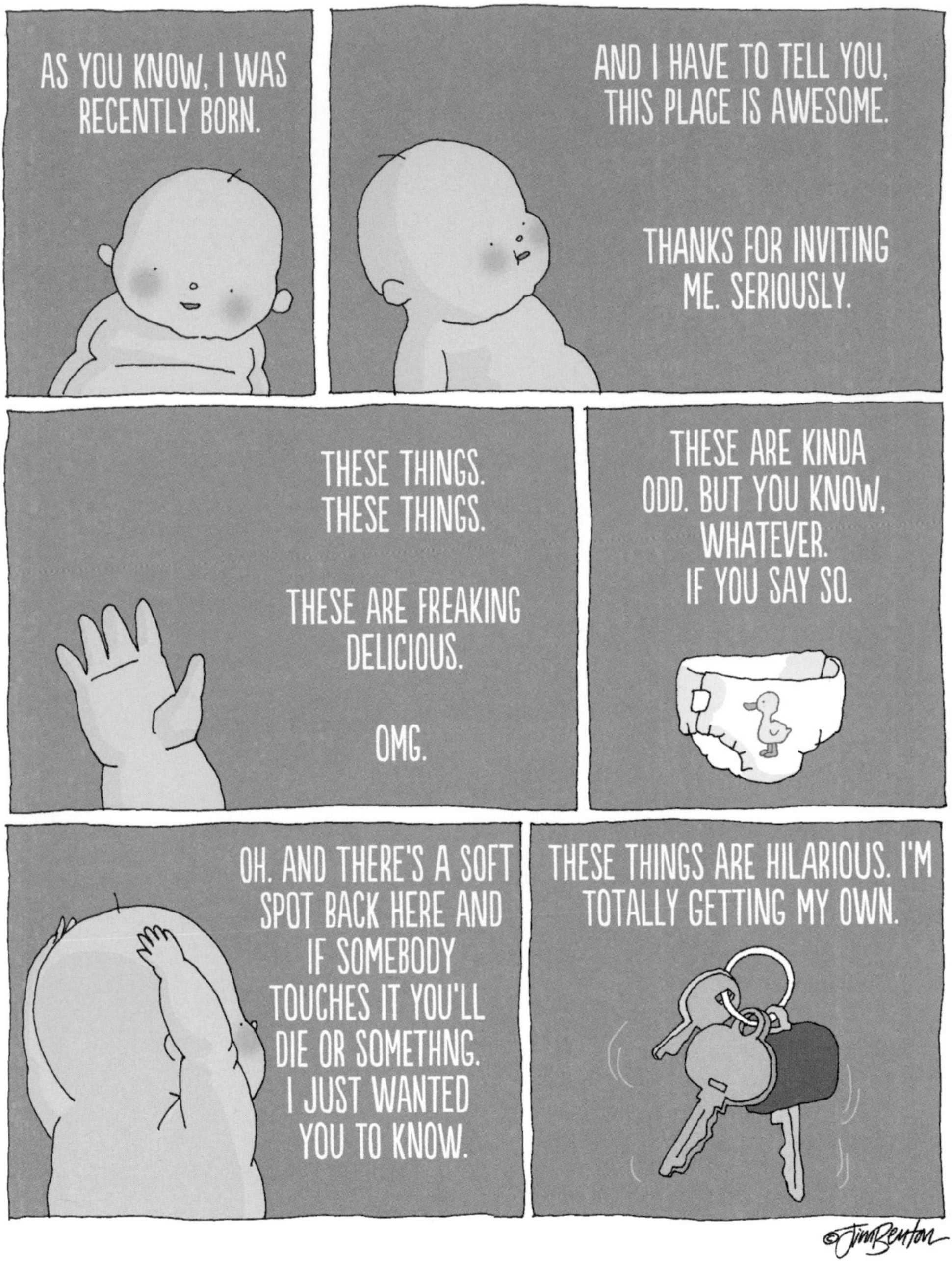
AS YOU KNOW, I WAS RECENTLY BORN.
AND I HAVE TO TELL YOU, THIS PLACE IS AWESOME.
THANKS FOR INVITING ME. SERIOUSLY.
THESE THINGS. THESE THINGS.
THESE ARE FREAKING DELICIOUS.
OMG.
THESE ARE KINDA ODD. BUT YOU KNOW, WHATEVER. IF YOU SAY SO.
OH. AND THERE'S A SOFT SPOT BACK HERE AND IF SOMEBODY TOUCHES IT YOU'LL DIE OR SOMETHNG. I JUST WANTED YOU TO KNOW.
THESE THINGS ARE HILARIOUS. I'M TOTALLY GETTING MY OWN.
©Jim Benton

The Teacher Pet

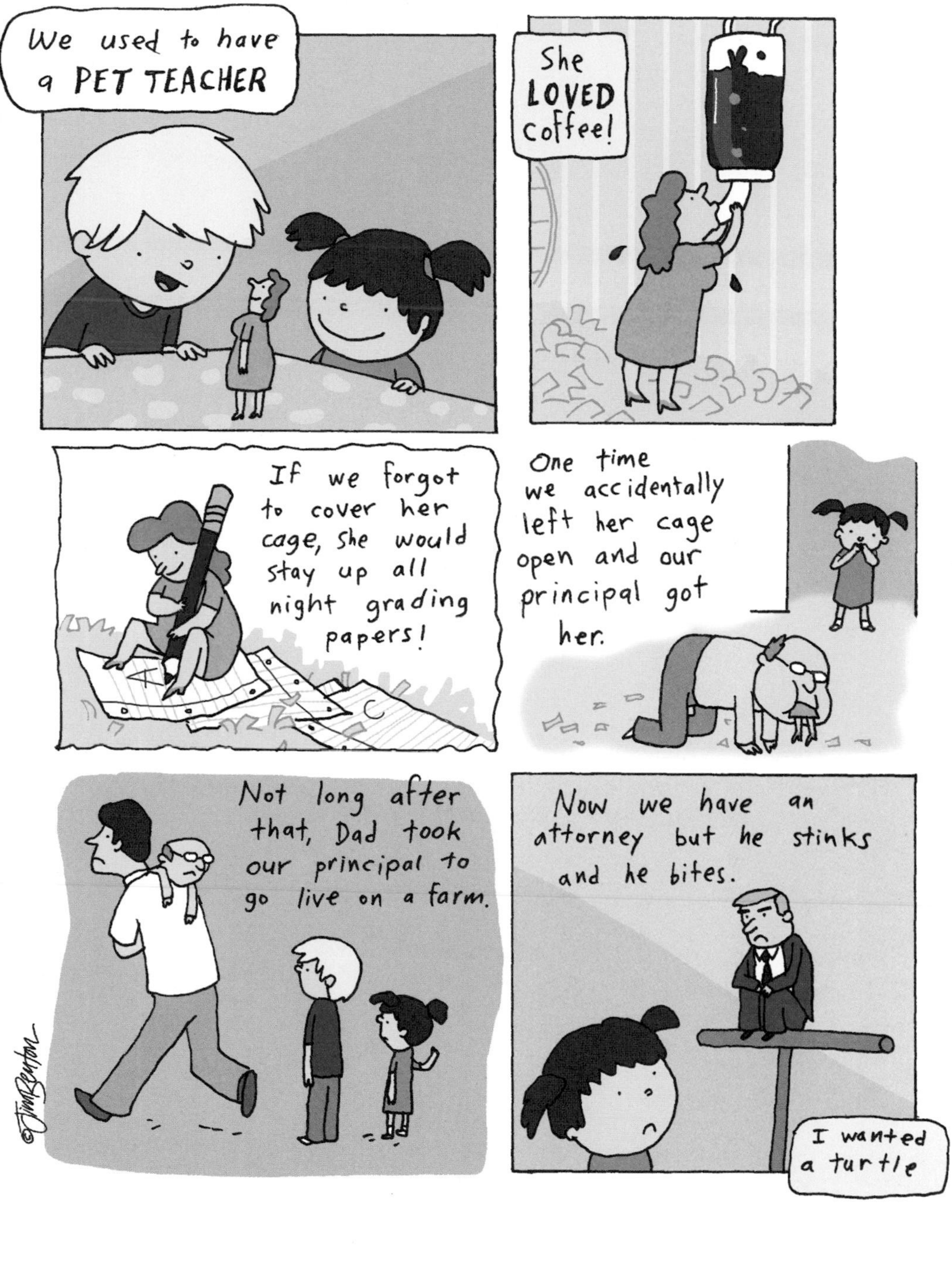

We used to have a PET TEACHER
She LOVED coffee!
If we forgot to cover her cage, she would stay up all night grading papers!
One time we accidentally left her cage open and our principal got her.
Not long after that, Dad took our principal to go live on a farm.
Now we have an attorney but he stinks and he bites.
I wanted a turtle
©Jim Benton

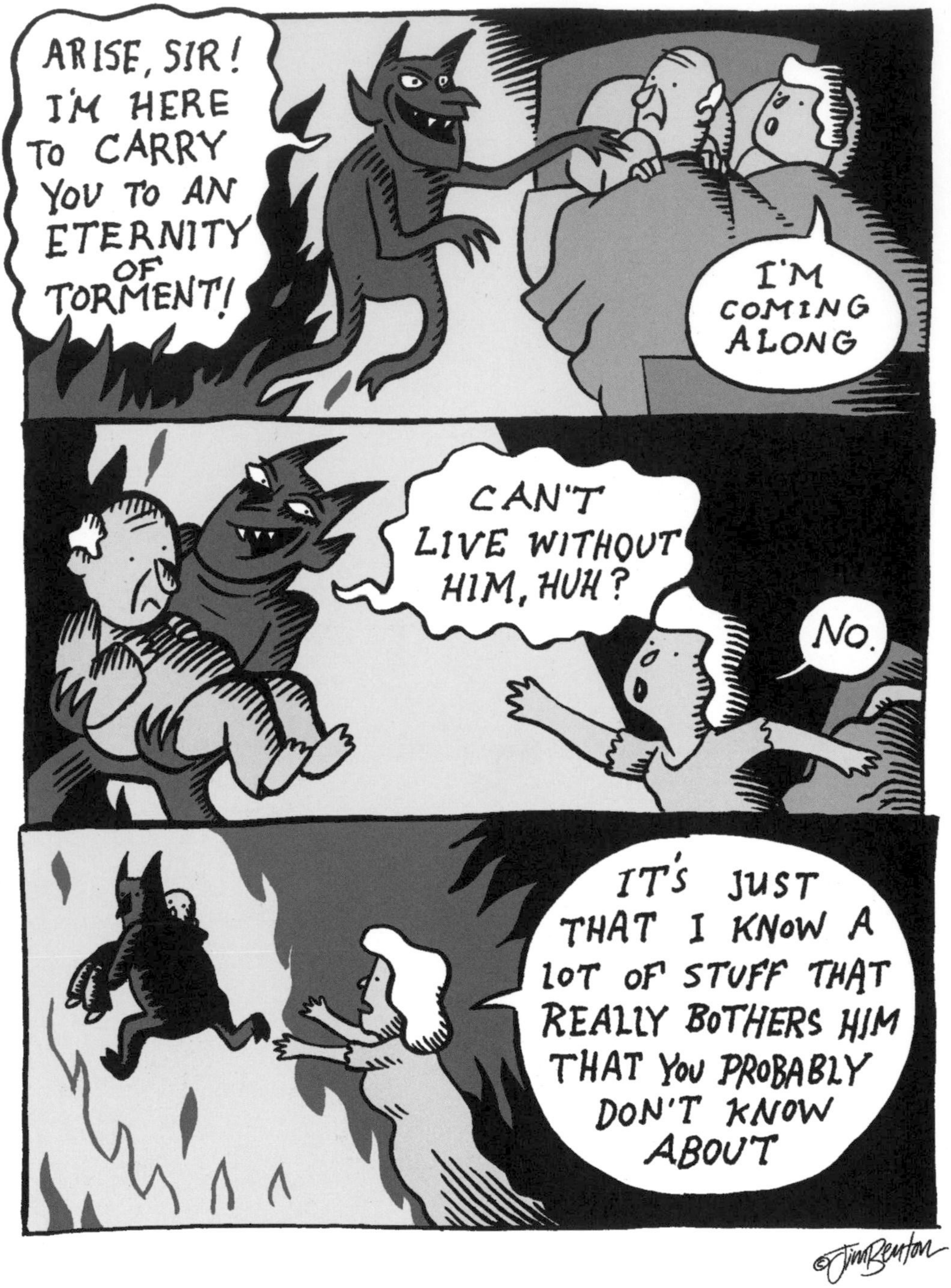
ARISE, SIR! I'M HERE TO CARRY YOU TO AN ETERNITY OF TORMENT!
I'M COMING ALONG
CAN'T LIVE WITHOUT HIM, HUH?
NO.
IT'S JUST THAT I KNOW A LOT OF STUFF THAT REALLY BOTHERS HIM THAT YOU PROBABLY DON'T KNOW ABOUT
©Jim Benton

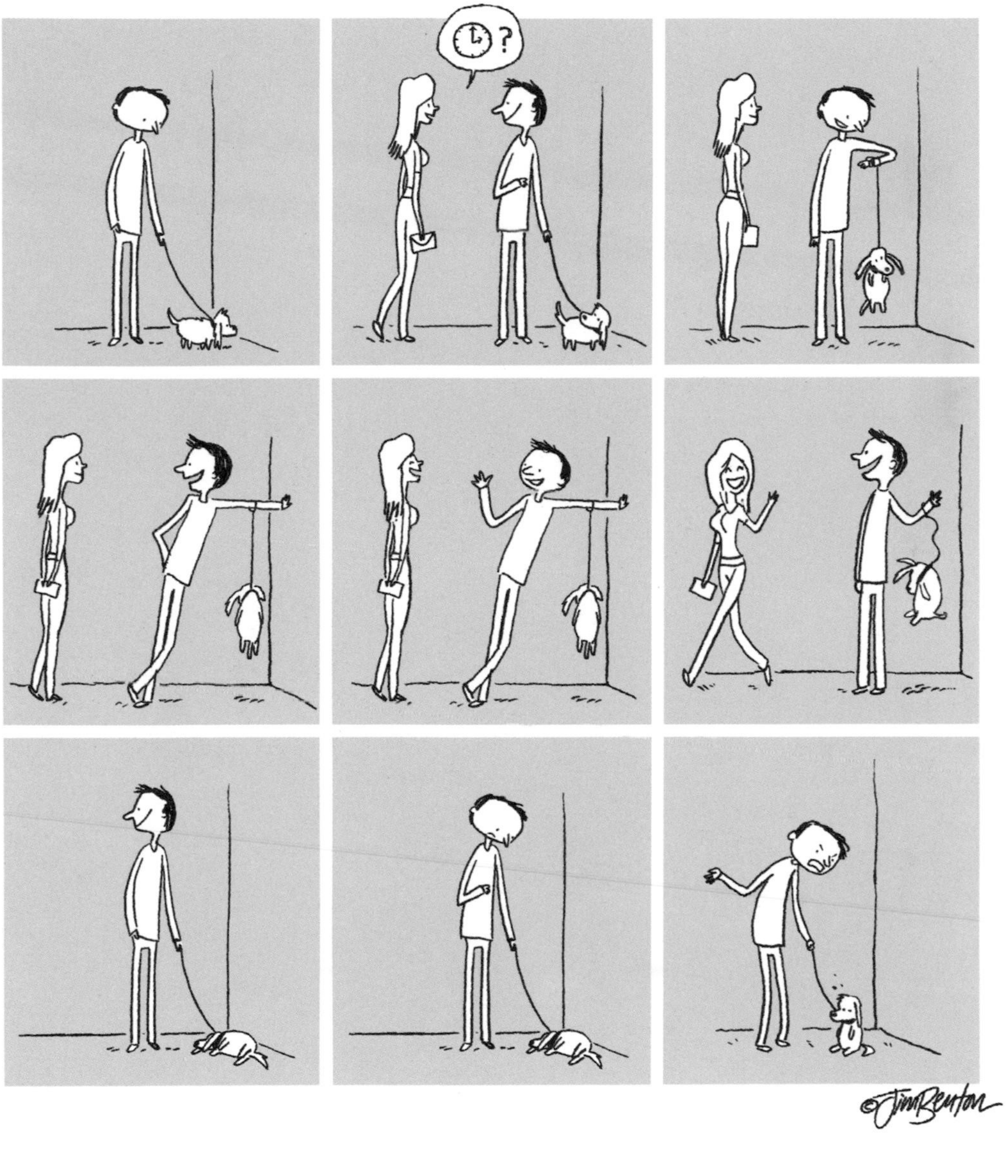
©Jim Benton

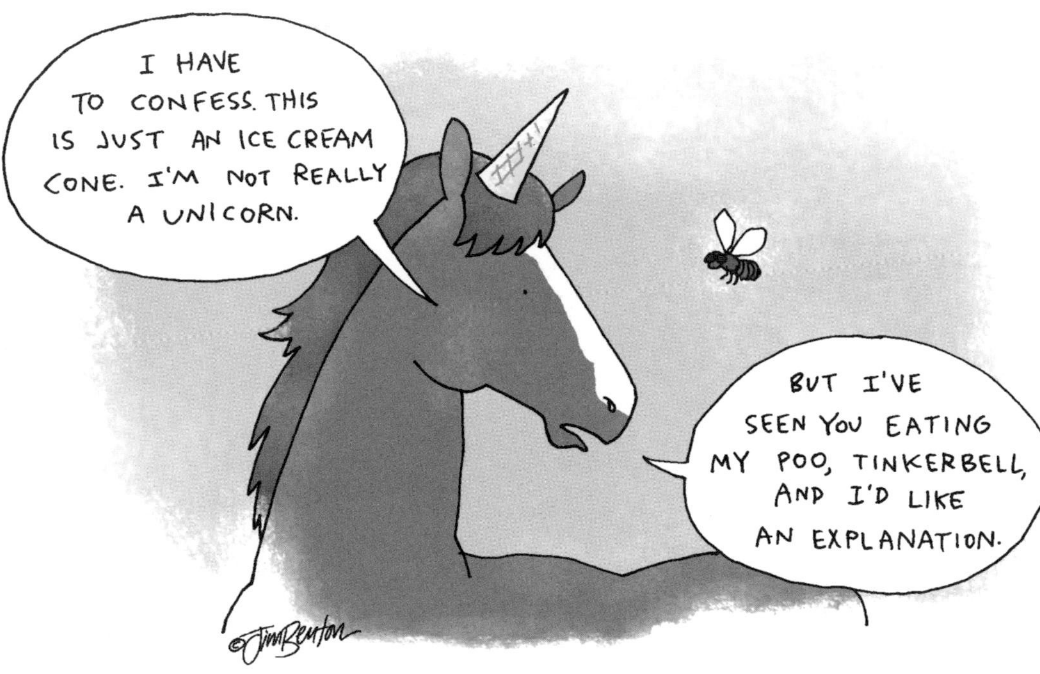
I HAVE TO CONFESS. THIS IS JUST AN ICE CREAM CONE. I'M NOT REALLY A UNICORN.
BUT I'VE SEEN YOU EATING MY POO, TINKERBELL, AND I'D LIKE AN EXPLANATION.
©Jim Benton

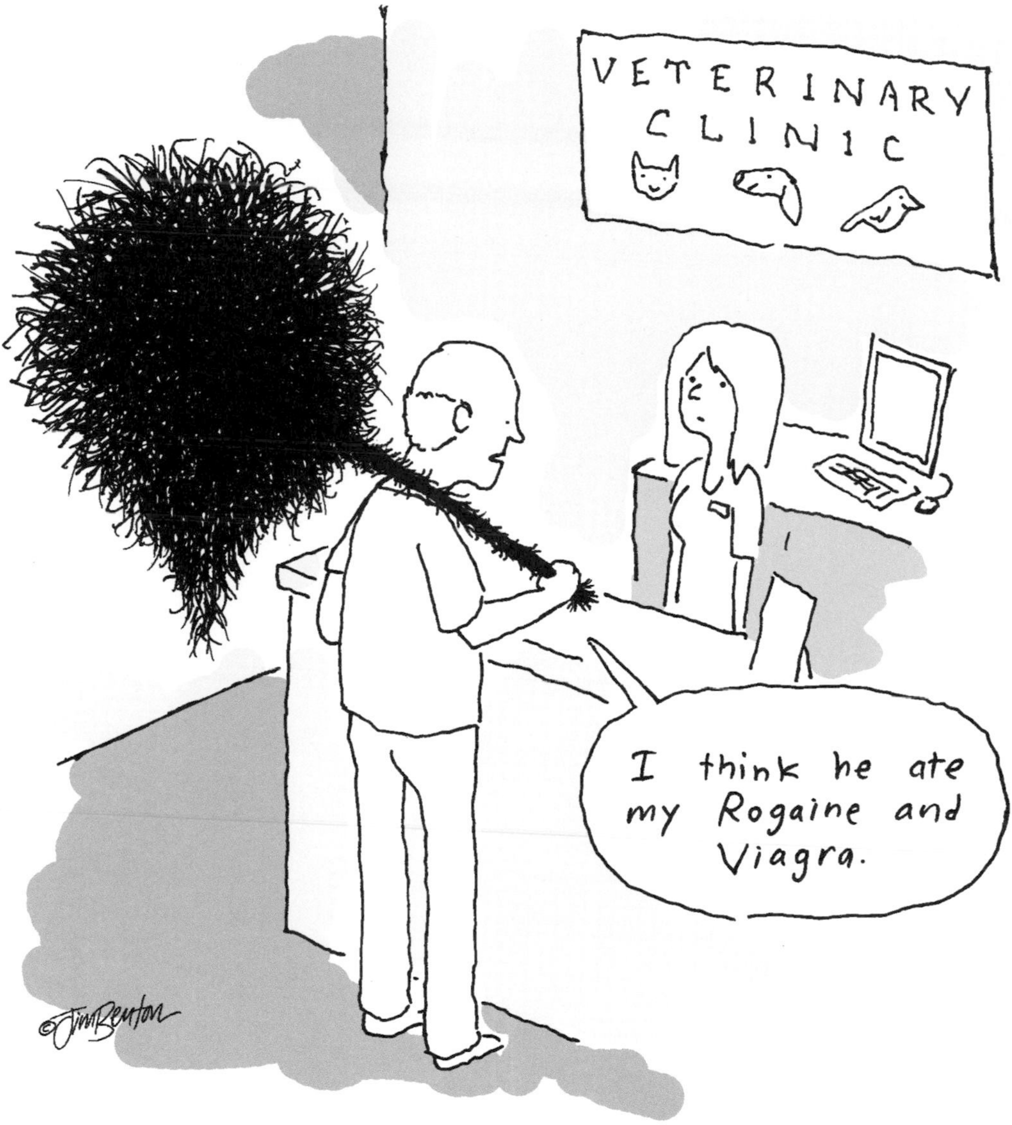
VETERINARY CLINIC
I think he ate my Rogaine and Viagra.
©Jim Benton

NEVER FORGET THAT
ALL YOU REALLY NEED IS
A SPRING IN YOUR STEP,
A SONG IN YOUR HEART,
AND A SHITLOAD OF CASH.

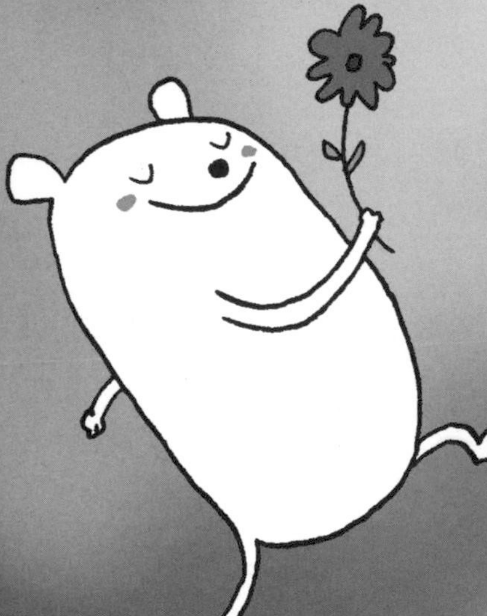
©Jim Benton

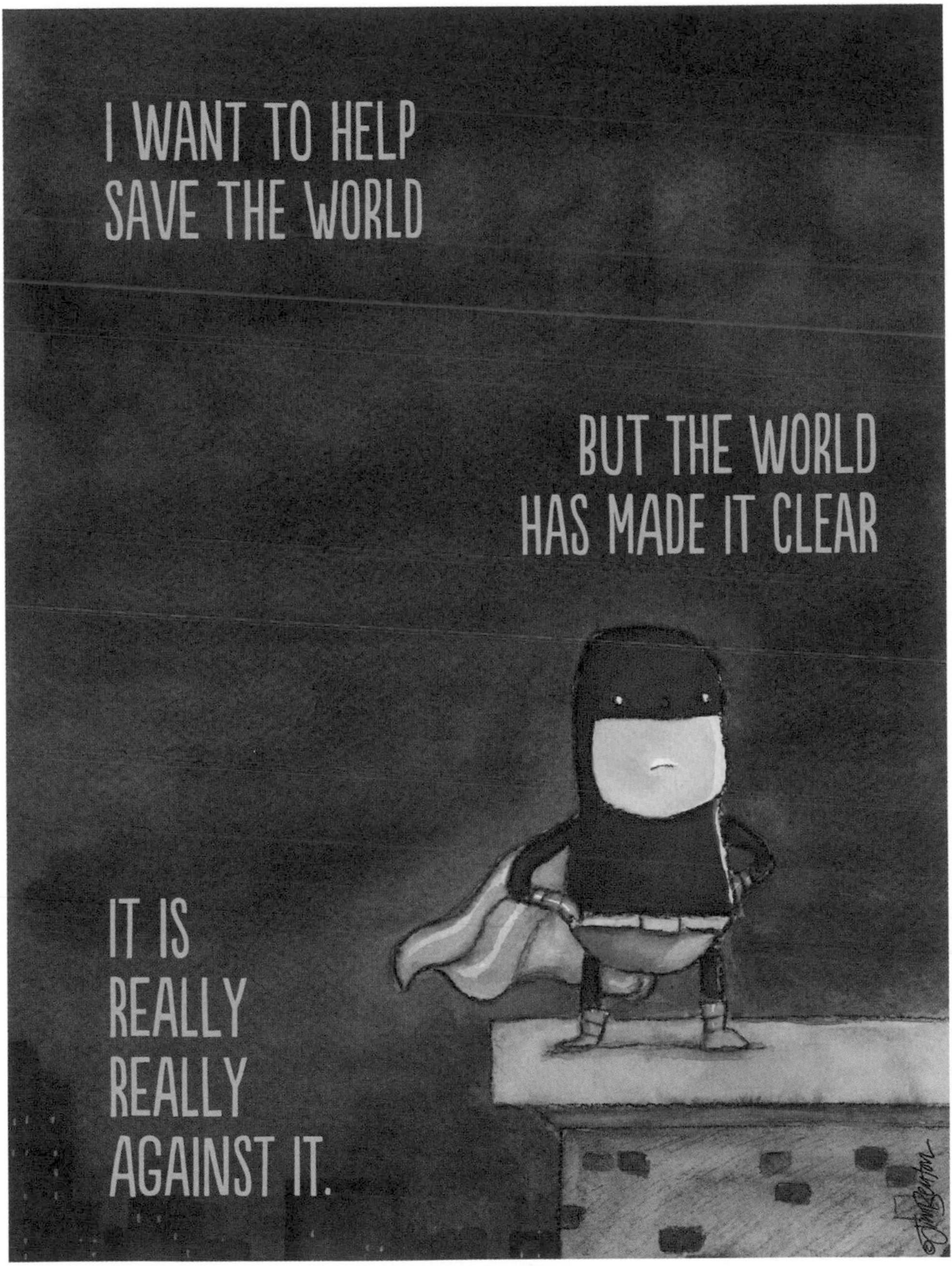
I WANT TO HELP
SAVE THE WORLD
BUT THE WORLD
HAS MADE IT CLEAR
IT IS
REALLY
REALLY
AGAINST IT.

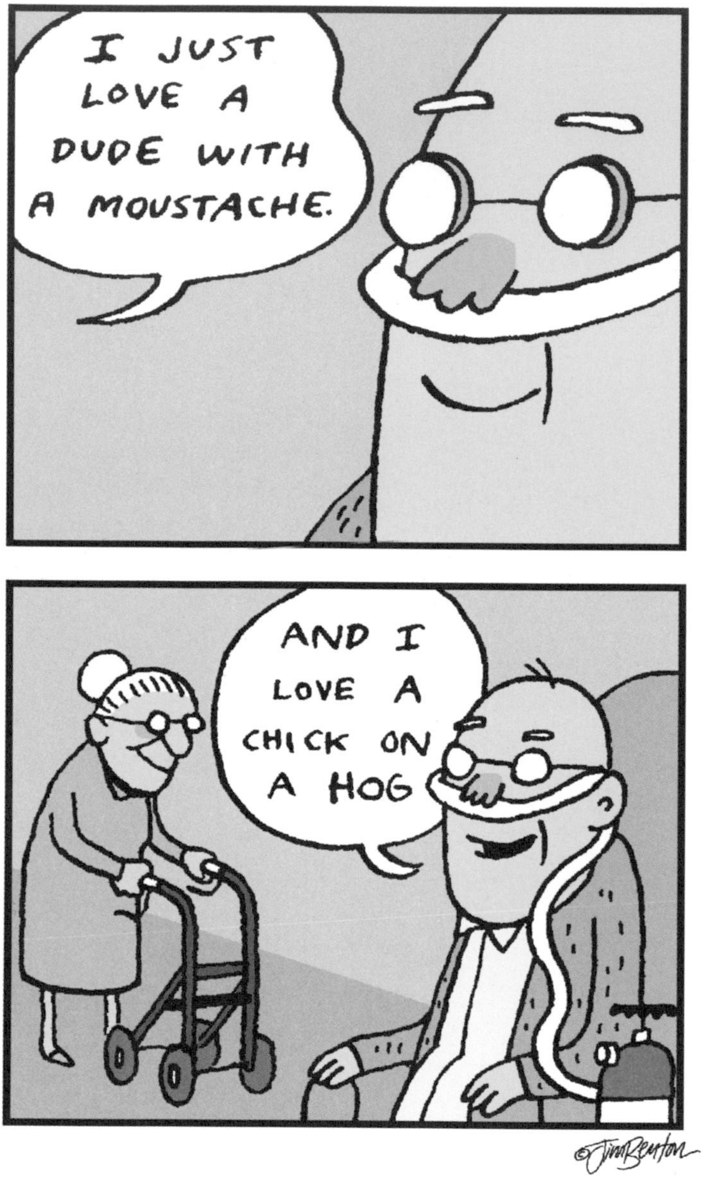
I JUST LOVE A DUDE WITH A MOUSTACHE.
AND I LOVE A CHICK ON A HOG
©Jim Benton

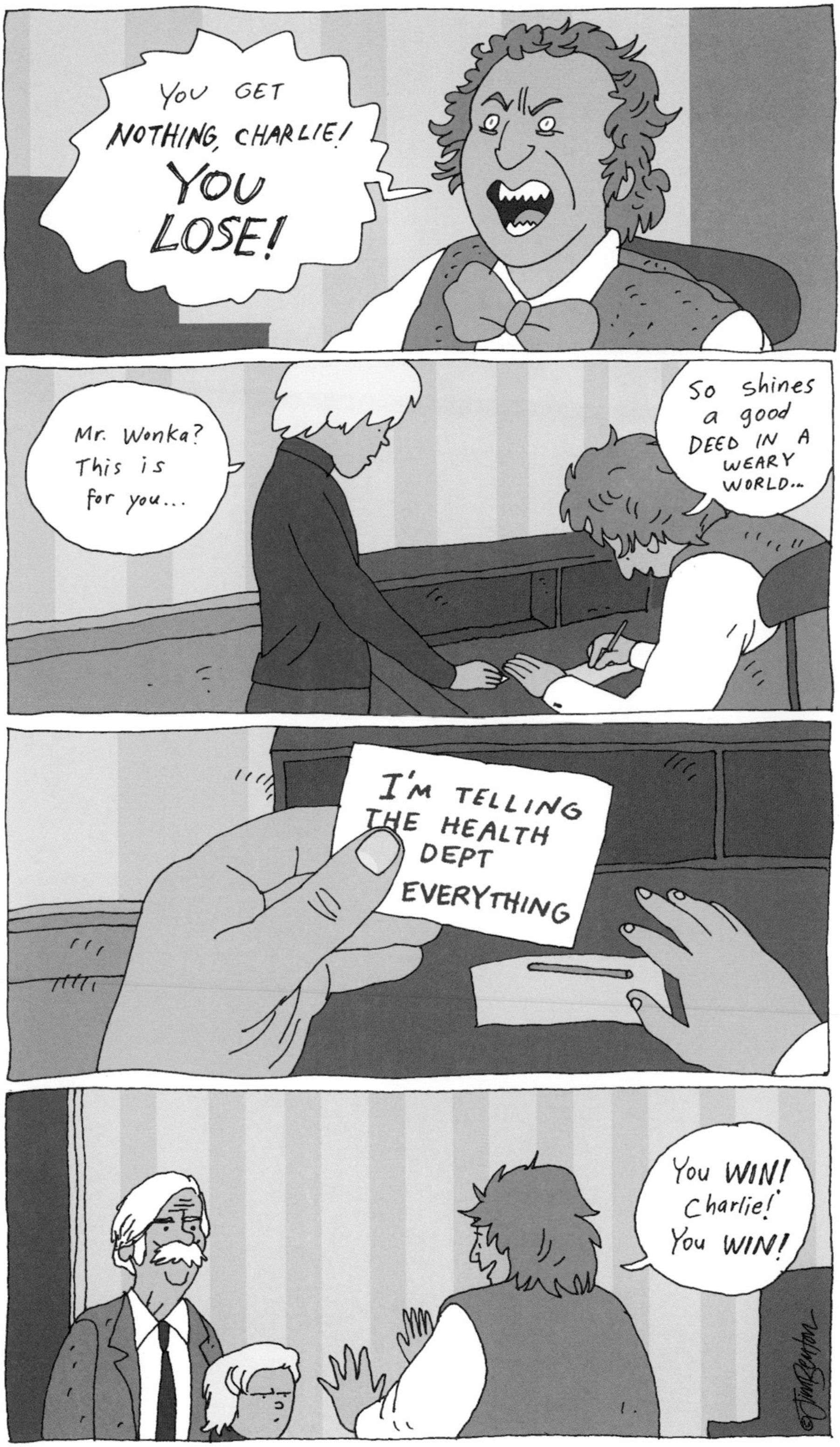
YOU GET NOTHING, CHARLIE! YOU LOSE!
Mr. Wonka? This is for you...
So shines a good DEED IN A WEARY WORLD...
I'M TELLING THE HEALTH DEPT EVERYTHING
You WIN! Charlie! You WIN!

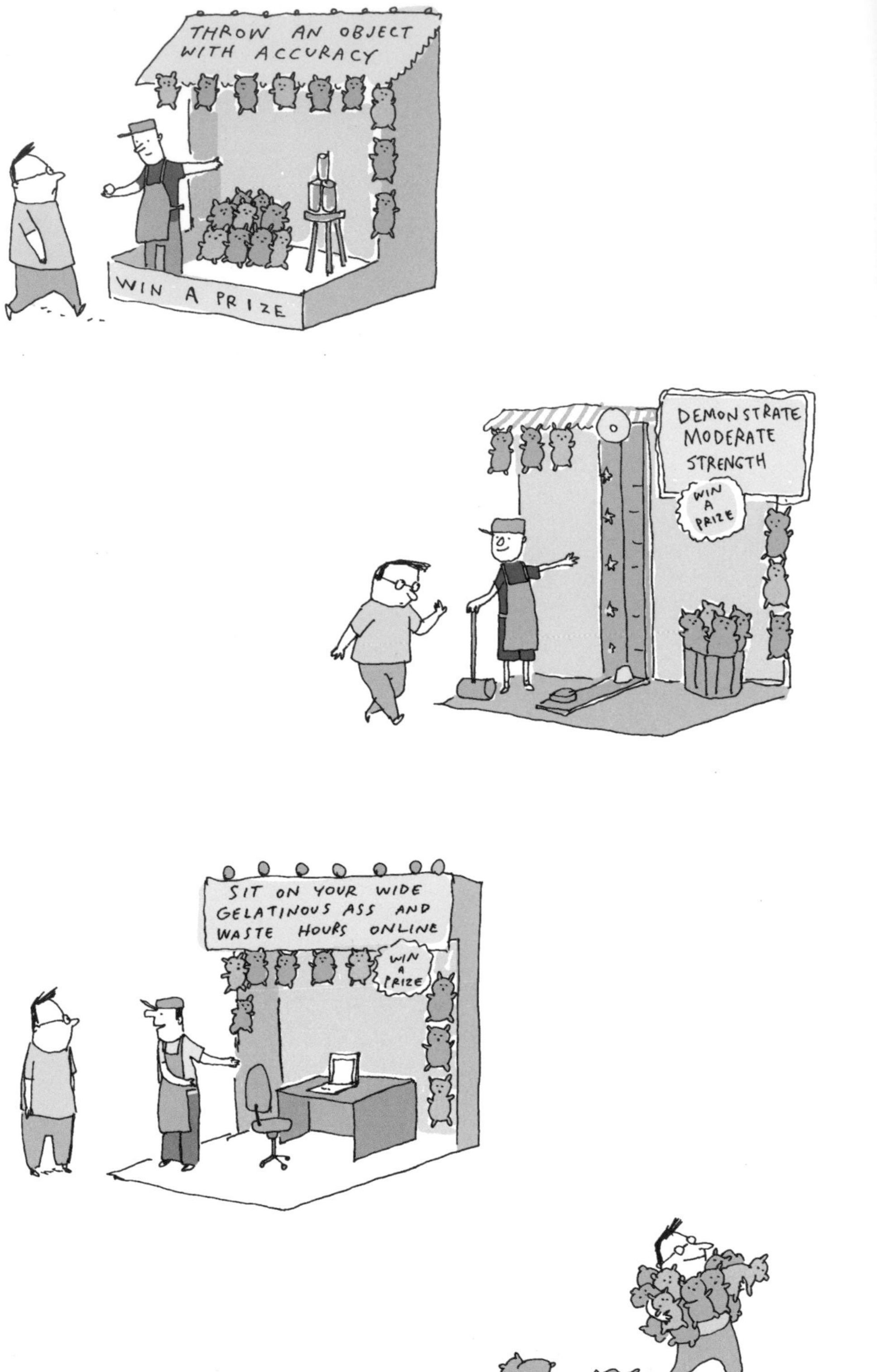
THROW AN OBJECT WITH ACCURACY
WIN A PRIZE
DEMONSTRATE MODERATE STRENGTH
WIN A PRIZE
SIT ON YOUR WIDE GELATINOUS ASS AND WASTE HOURS ONLINE
WIN A PRIZE
©Jim Benton

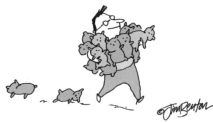

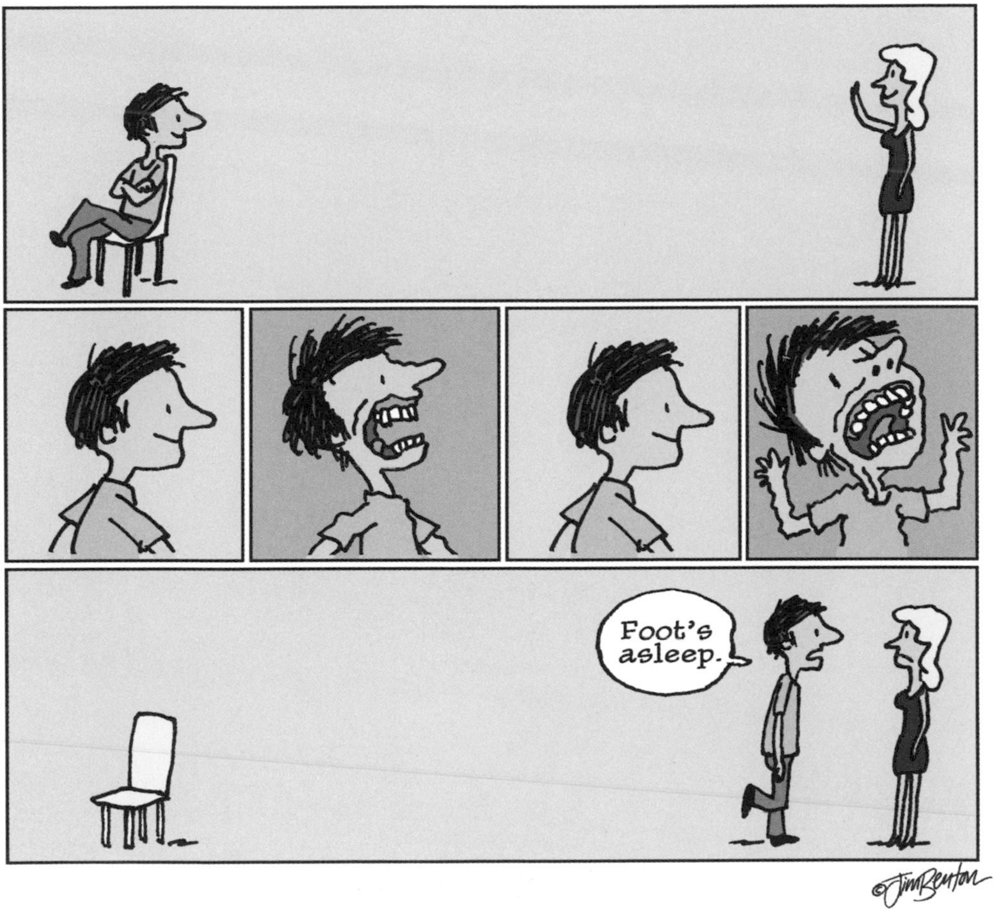
Foot's asleep.
©Jim Benton

HA HAHA WHAT NOW?

THUNK

STOMP
STOMP
STOMP
STOMP

VROOM VROOM

SQUEEEEEEEEE

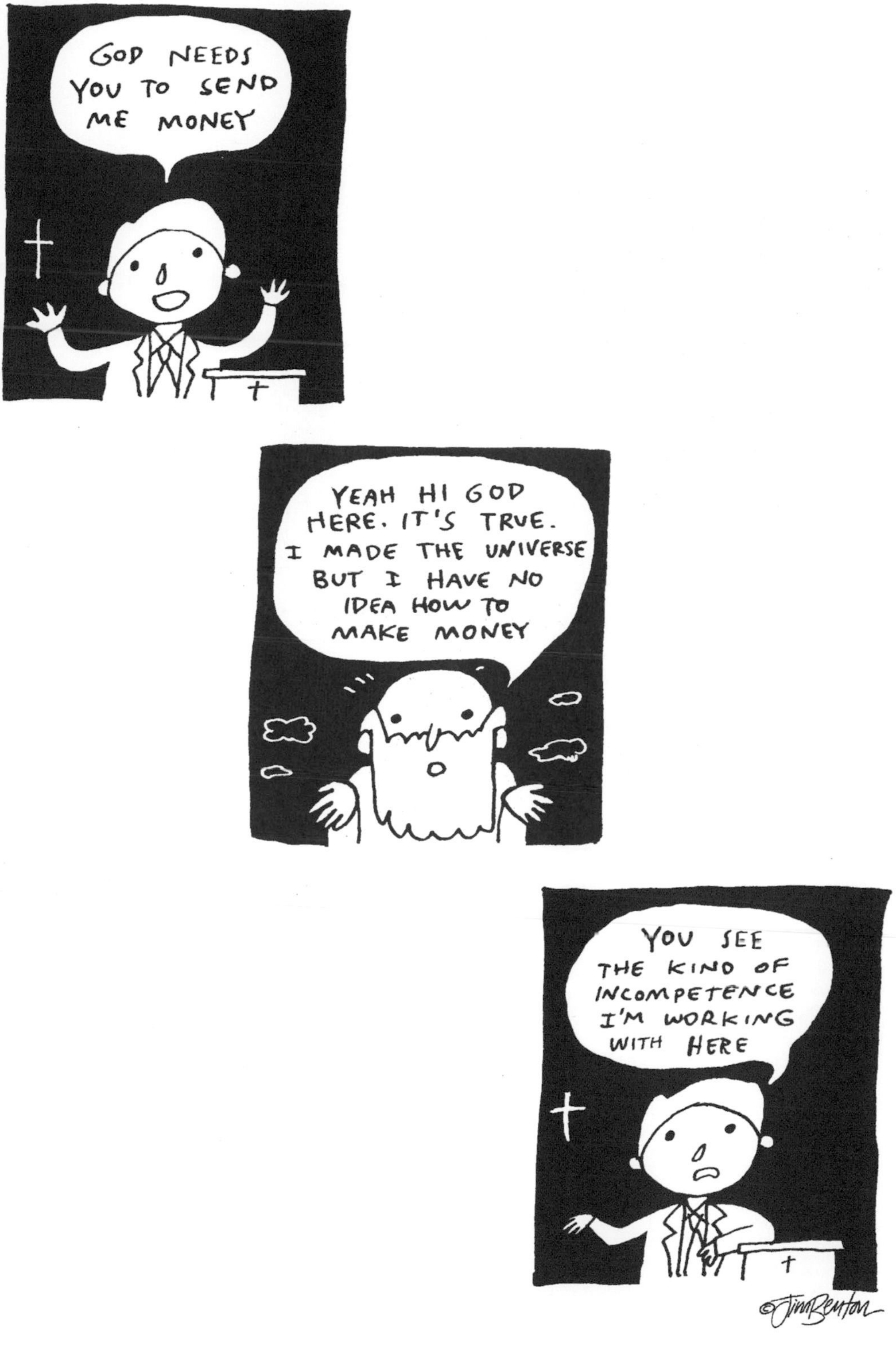
GOD NEEDS YOU TO SEND ME MONEY
YEAH HI GOD HERE. IT'S TRUE. I MADE THE UNIVERSE BUT I HAVE NO IDEA HOW TO MAKE MONEY
YOU SEE THE KIND OF INCOMPETENCE I'M WORKING WITH HERE
©Jim Benton

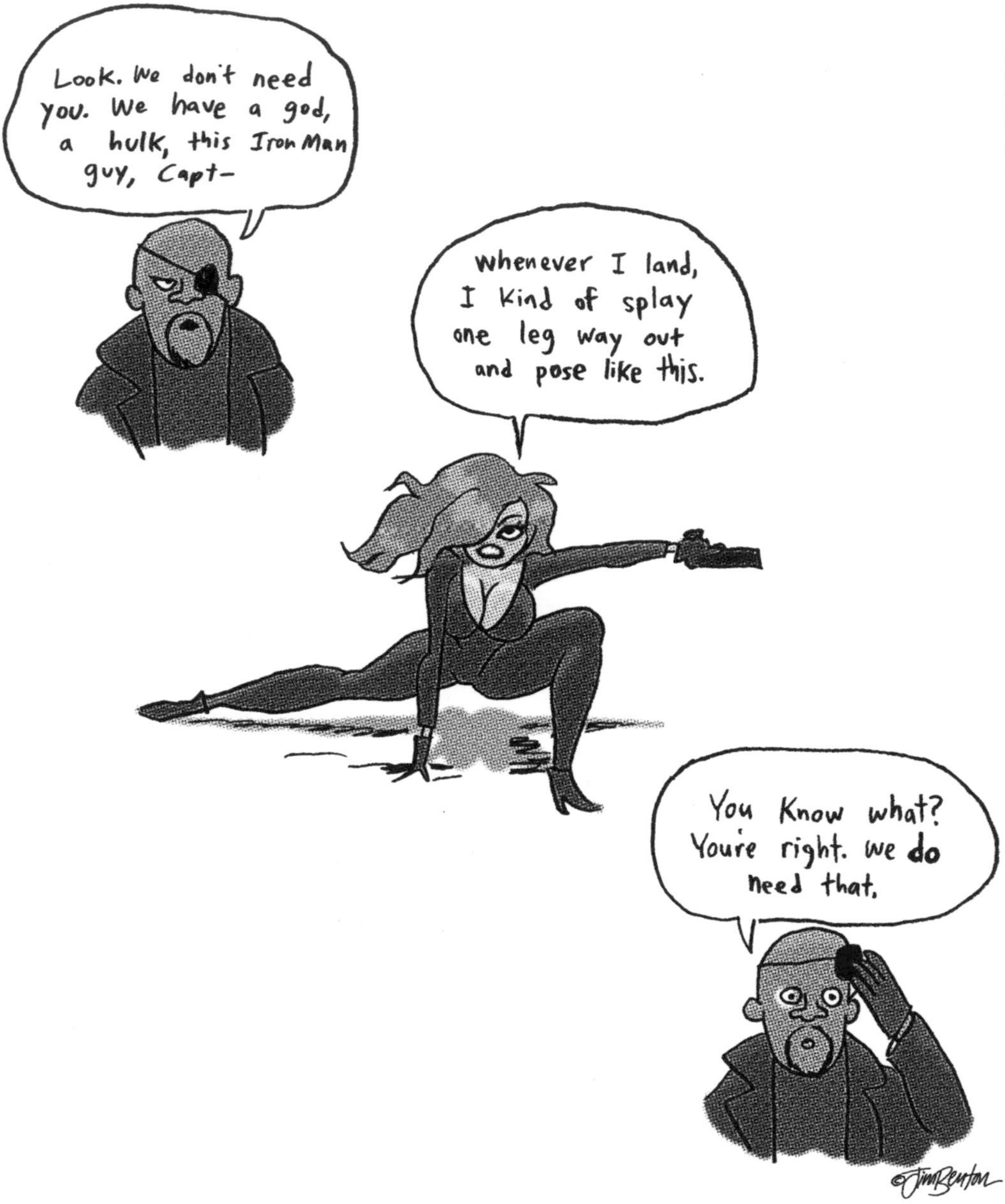
Look. We don't need you. We have a god, a hulk, this Iron Man guy, Capt-
Whenever I land, I kind of splay one leg way out and pose like this.
You Know what? You're right. we do need that.
©Jim Benton

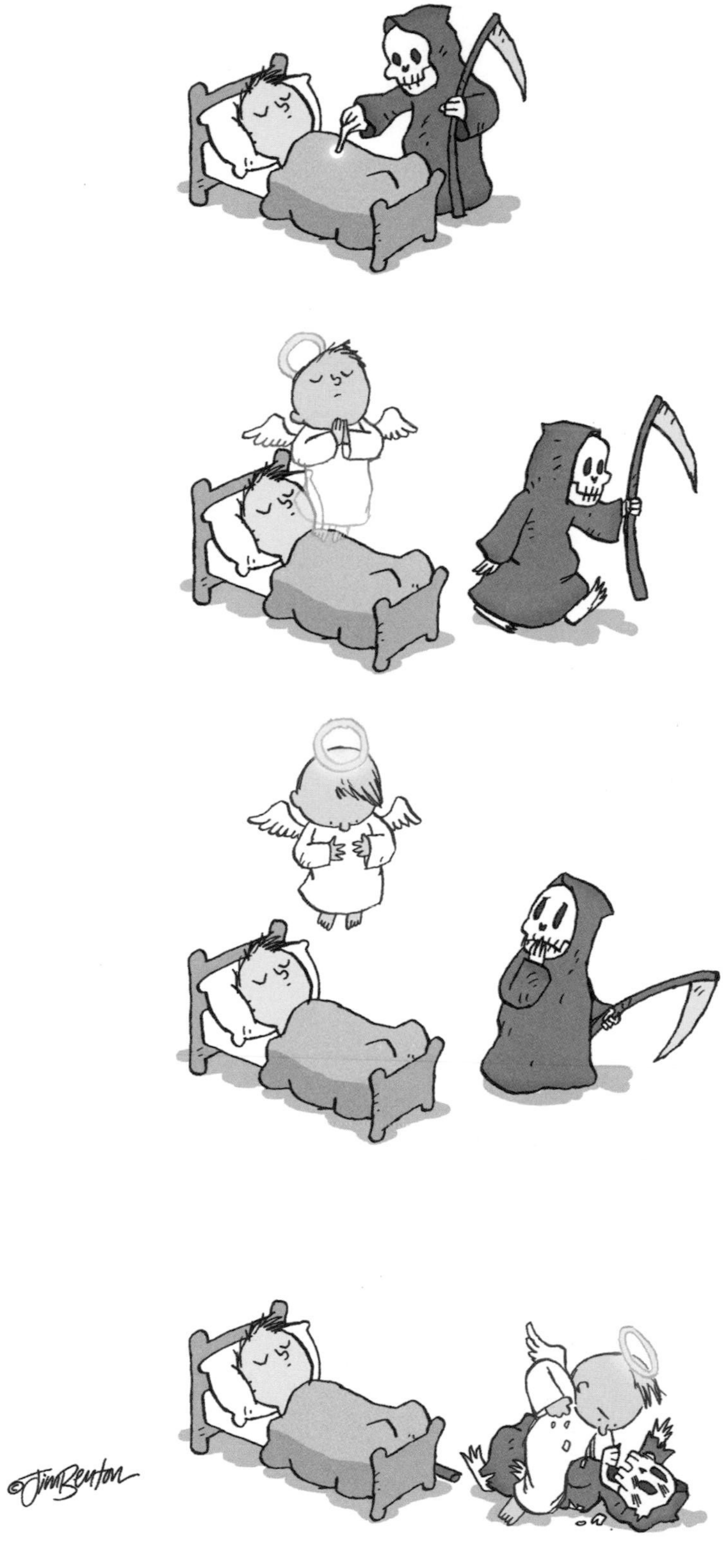
©Jim Benton

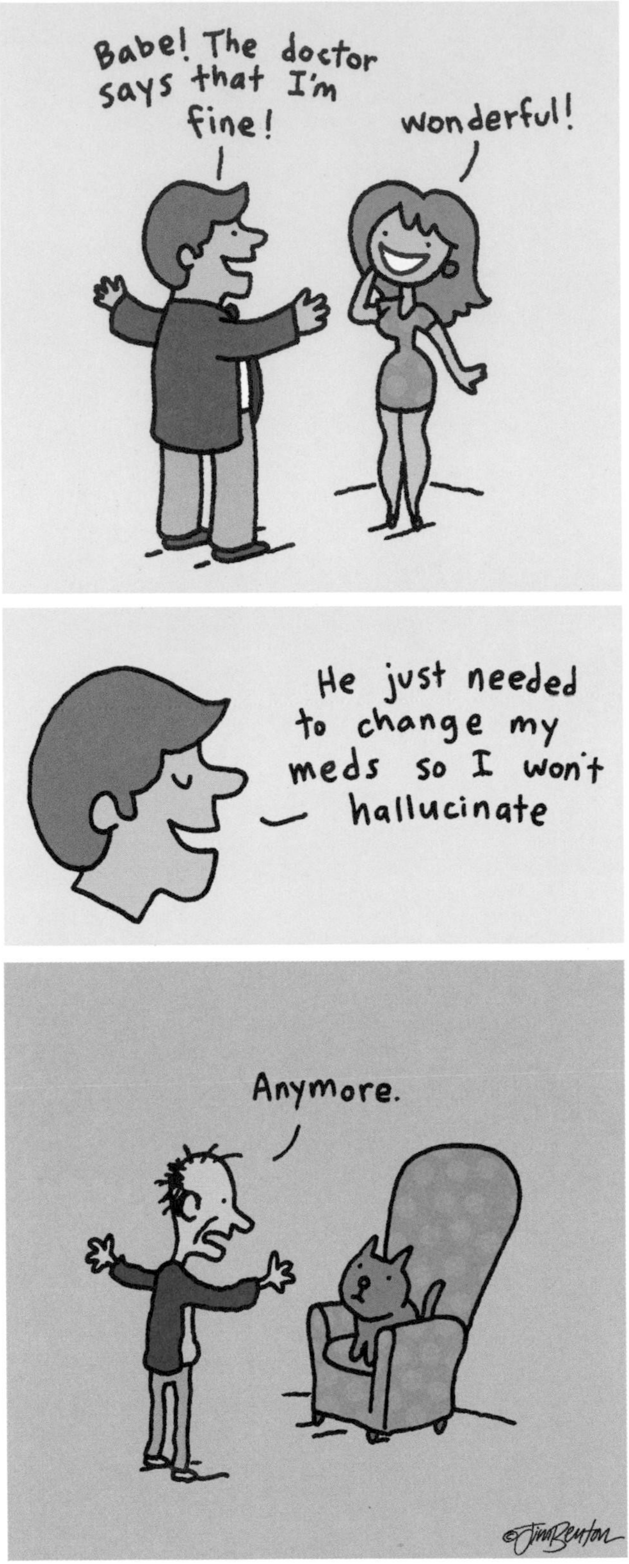
Babe! The doctor says that I'm fine!
wonderful!
He just needed to change my meds so I won't hallucinate
Anymore.
©Jim Benton

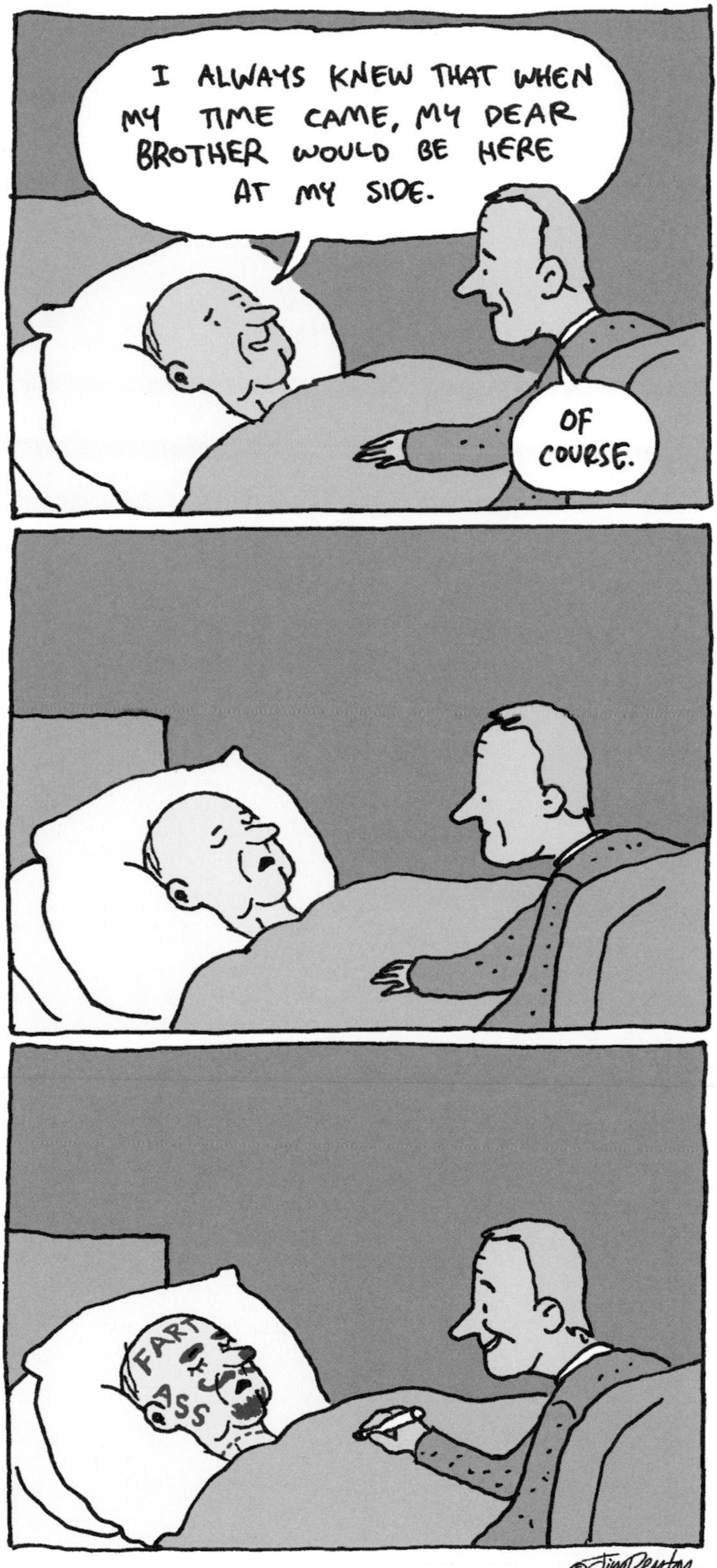
I ALWAYS KNEW THAT WHEN MY TIME CAME, MY DEAR BROTHER WOULD BE HERE AT MY SIDE.
OF COURSE.
FART
ASS
©Jim Benton

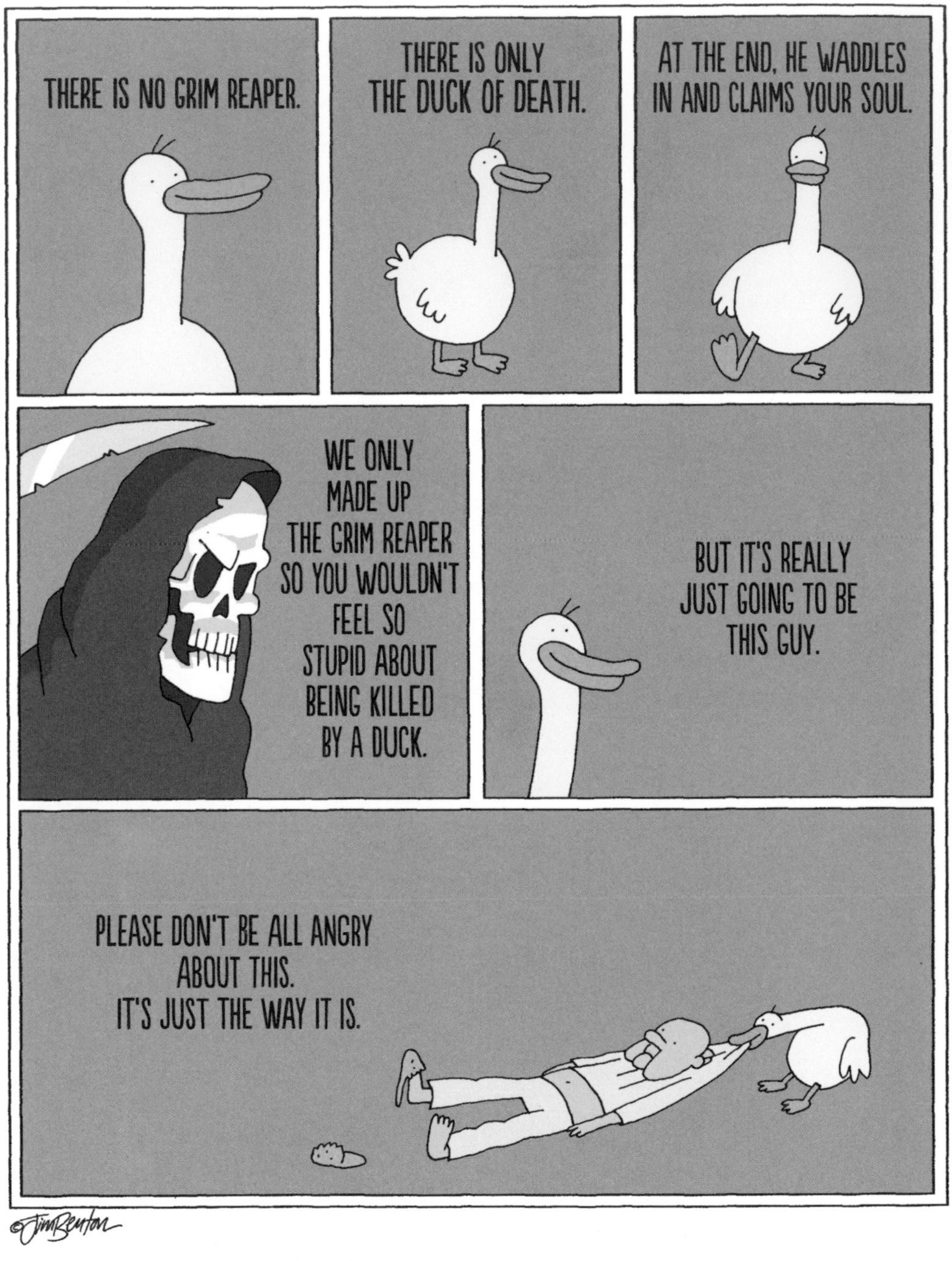
THERE IS NO GRIM REAPER.
THERE IS ONLY THE DUCK OF DEATH.
AT THE END, HE WADDLES IN AND CLAIMS YOUR SOUL.
WE ONLY MADE UP THE GRIM REAPER SO YOU WOULDN'T FEEL SO STUPID ABOUT BEING KILLED BY A DUCK.
BUT IT'S REALLY JUST GOING TO BE THIS GUY.
PLEASE DON'T BE ALL ANGRY ABOUT THIS.
IT'S JUST THE WAY IT IS.

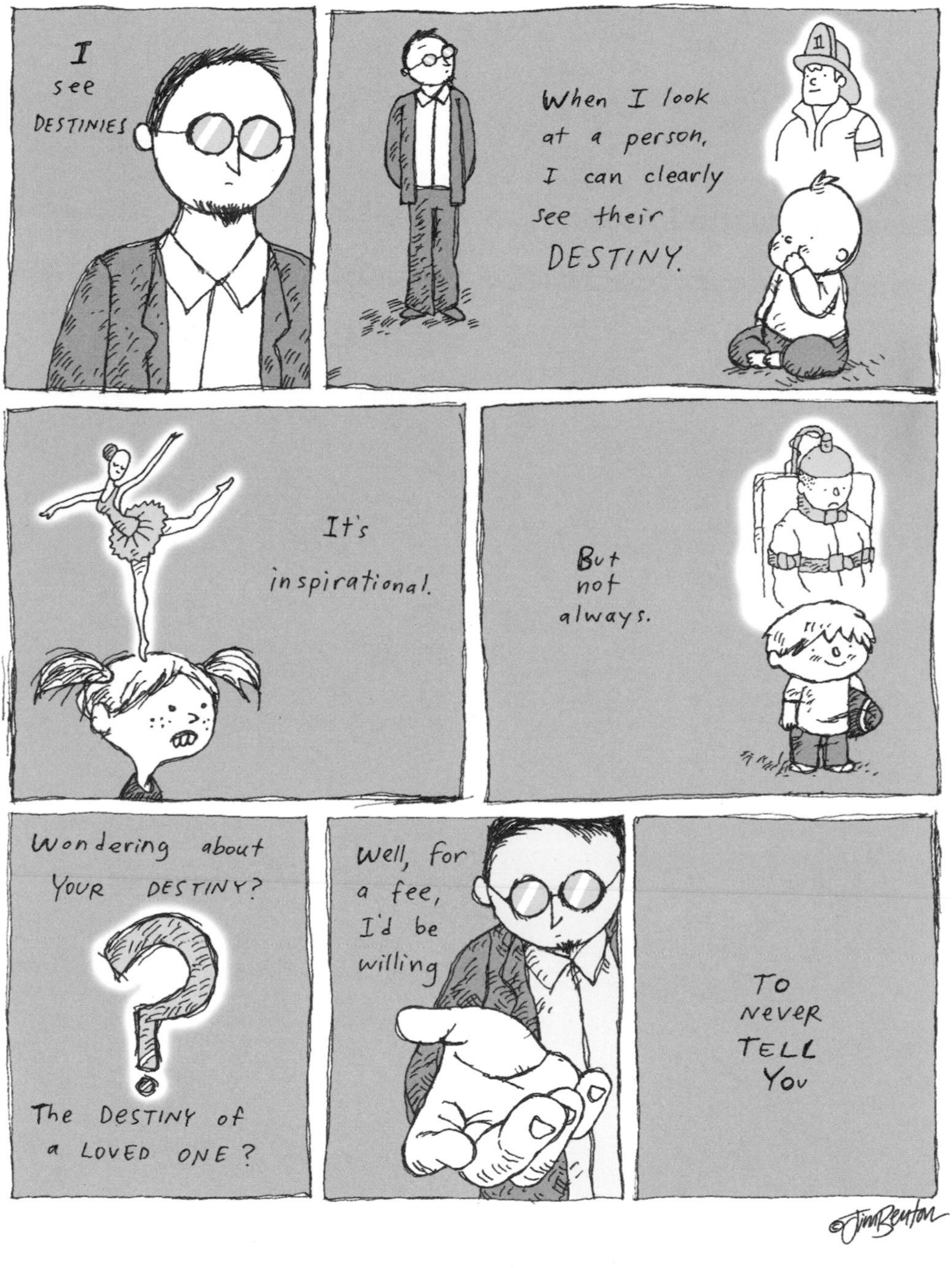
I see DESTINIES
When I look at a person, I can clearly see their DESTINY.
It's inspirational.
But not always.
Wondering about YOUR DESTINY?
The DESTINY of a LOVED ONE?
Well, for a fee, I'd be willing
TO NEVER TELL YOU
©Jim Benton

Observational Comedy

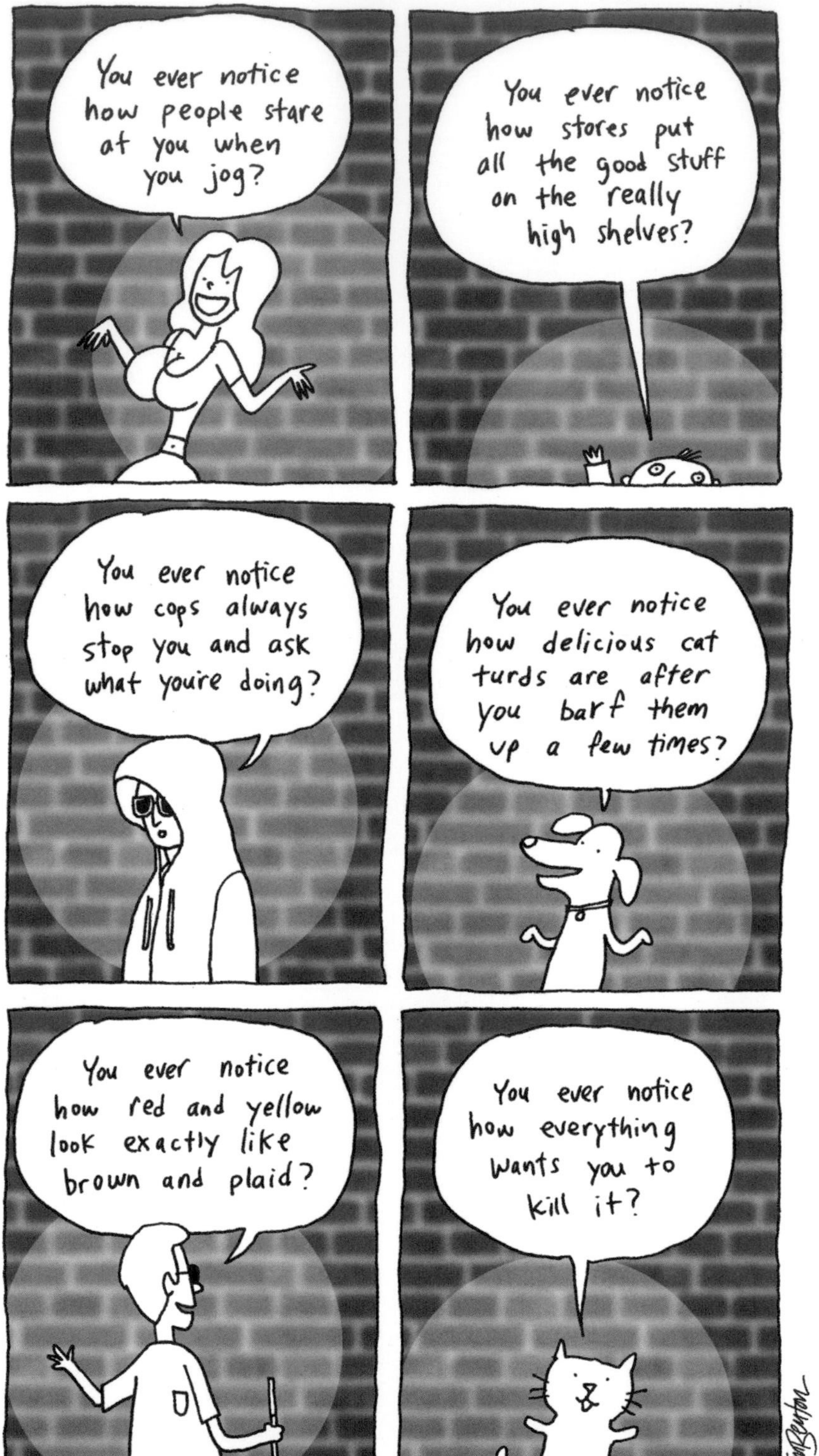

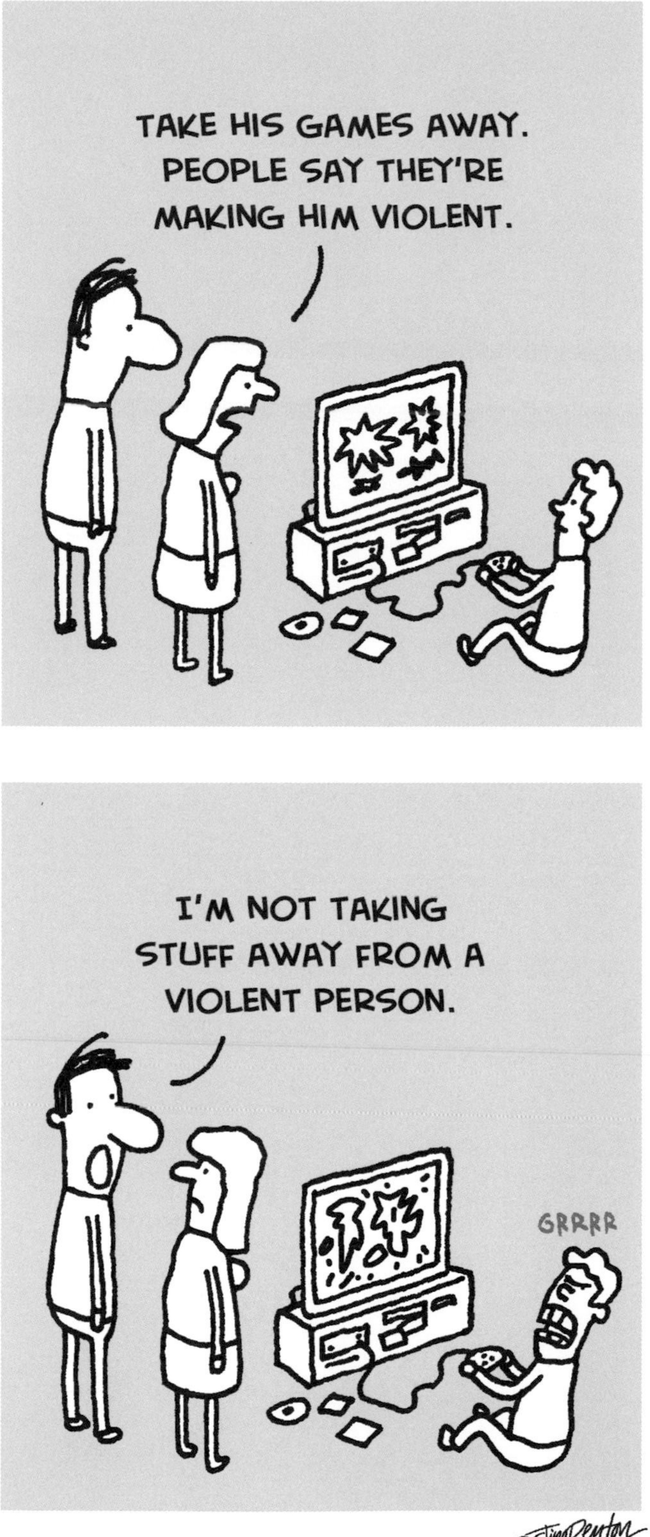
TAKE HIS GAMES AWAY. PEOPLE SAY THEY'RE MAKING HIM VIOLENT.
I'M NOT TAKING STUFF AWAY FROM A VIOLENT PERSON.
GRRRR
©Jim Benton

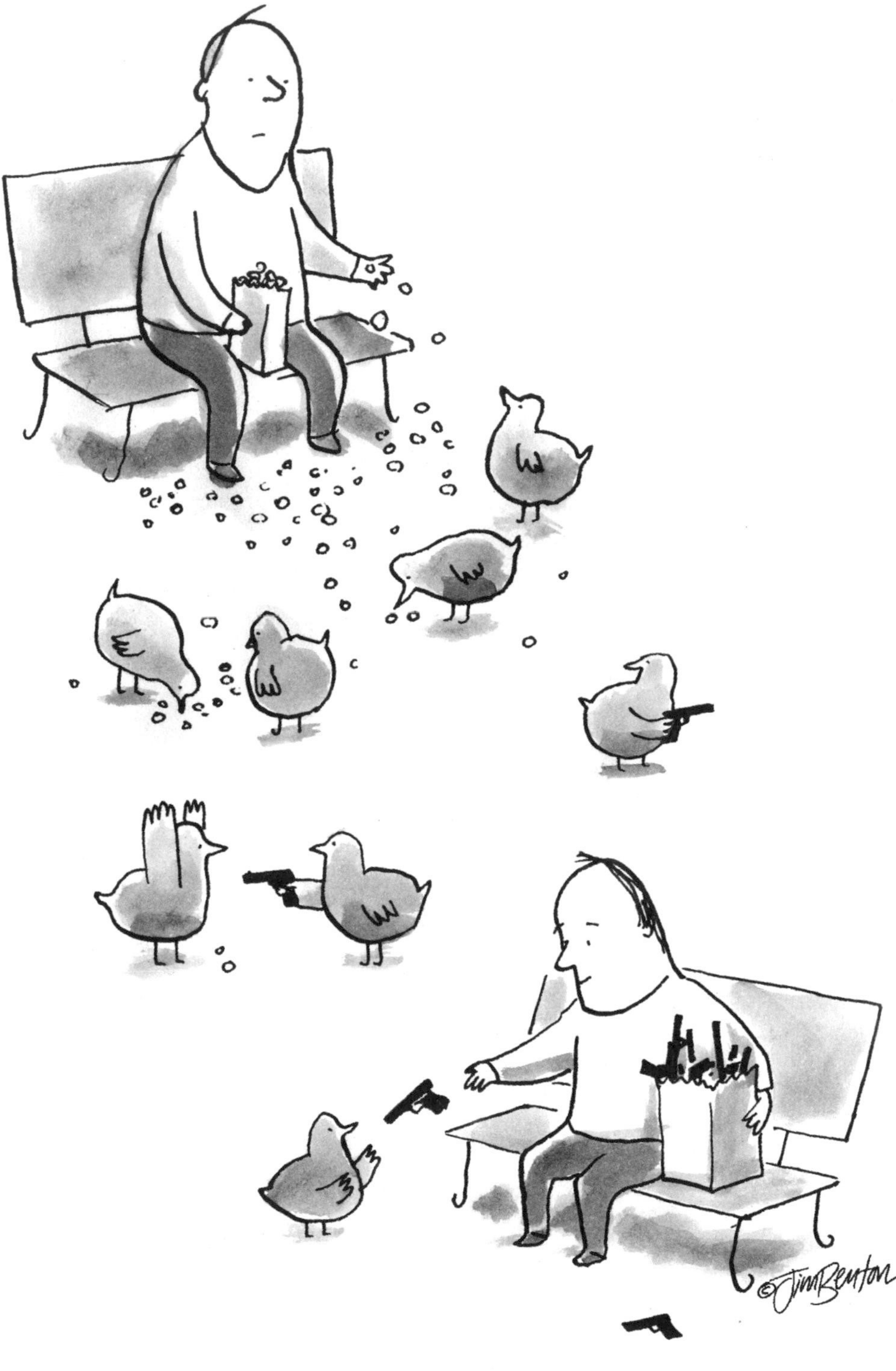
©Jim Benton

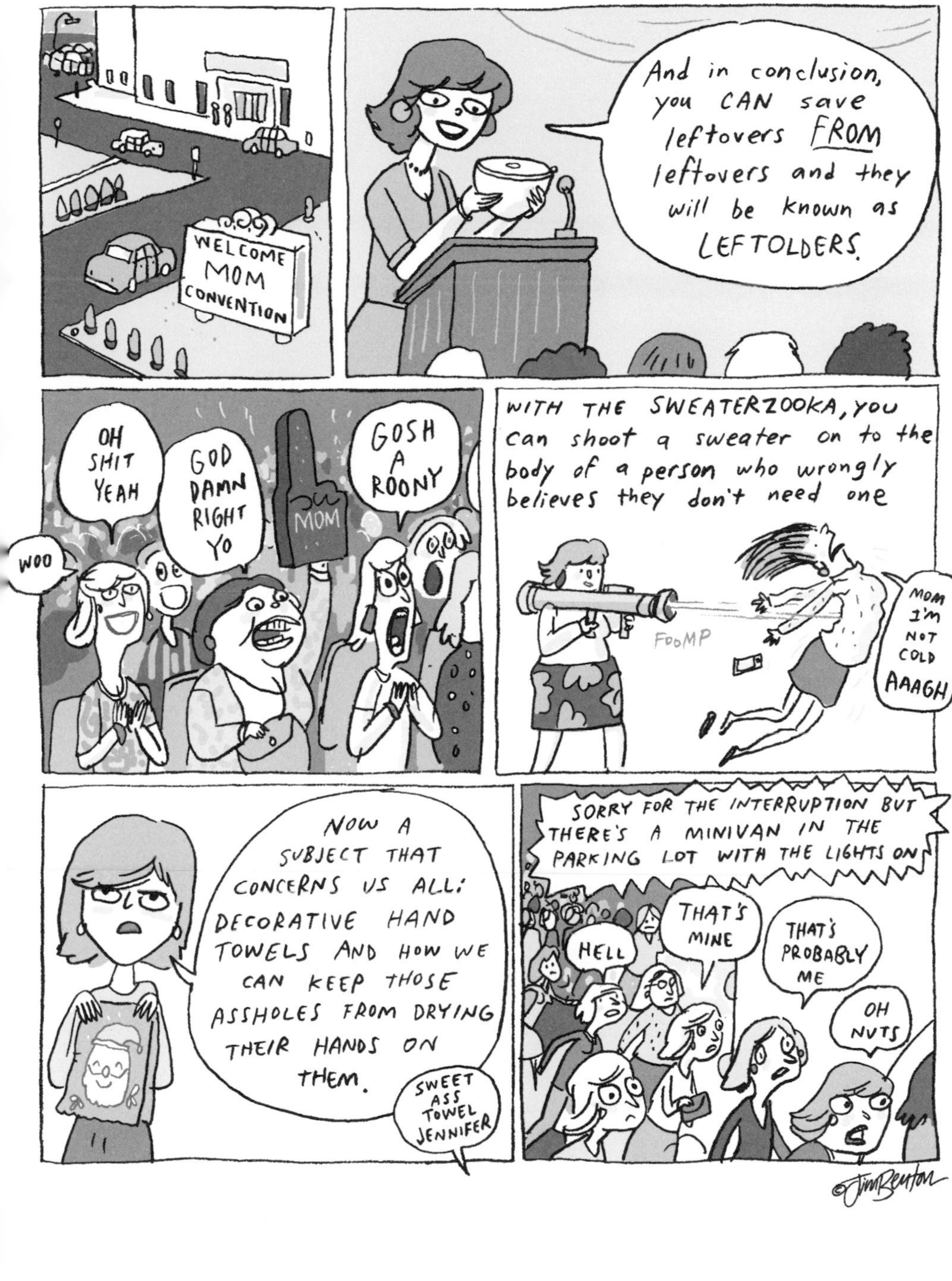
WELCOME MOM CONVENTION
And in conclusion, you CAN save leftovers FROM leftovers and they will be known as LEFTOLDERS.
WOO
OH SHIT YEAH
GOD DAMN RIGHT YO
MOM
GOSH A ROONY
WITH THE SWEATERZOOKA, YOU can shoot a sweater on to the body of a person who wrongly believes they don't need one
FOOMP
MOM I'M NOT COLD AAAGH
NOW A SUBJECT THAT CONCERNS US ALL: DECORATIVE HAND TOWELS AND HOW WE CAN KEEP THOSE ASSHOLES FROM DRYING THEIR HANDS ON THEM.
SWEET ASS TOWEL JENNIFER
SORRY FOR THE INTERRUPTION BUT THERE'S A MINIVAN IN THE PARKING LOT WITH THE LIGHTS ON
HELL
THAT'S MINE
THAT'S PROBABLY ME
OH NUTS
©Jim Benton

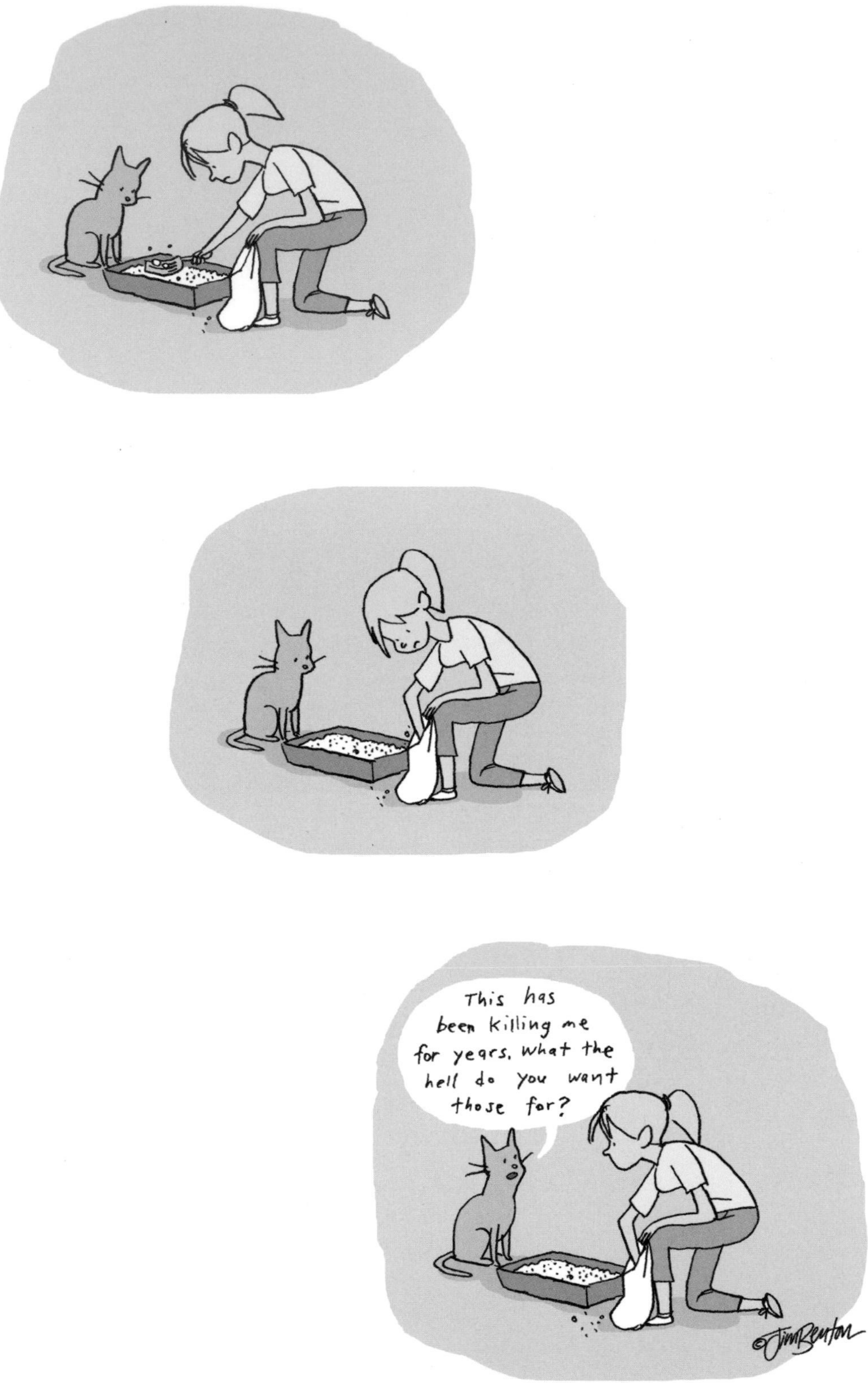
This has been killing me for years. What the hell do you want those for?
©Jim Benton

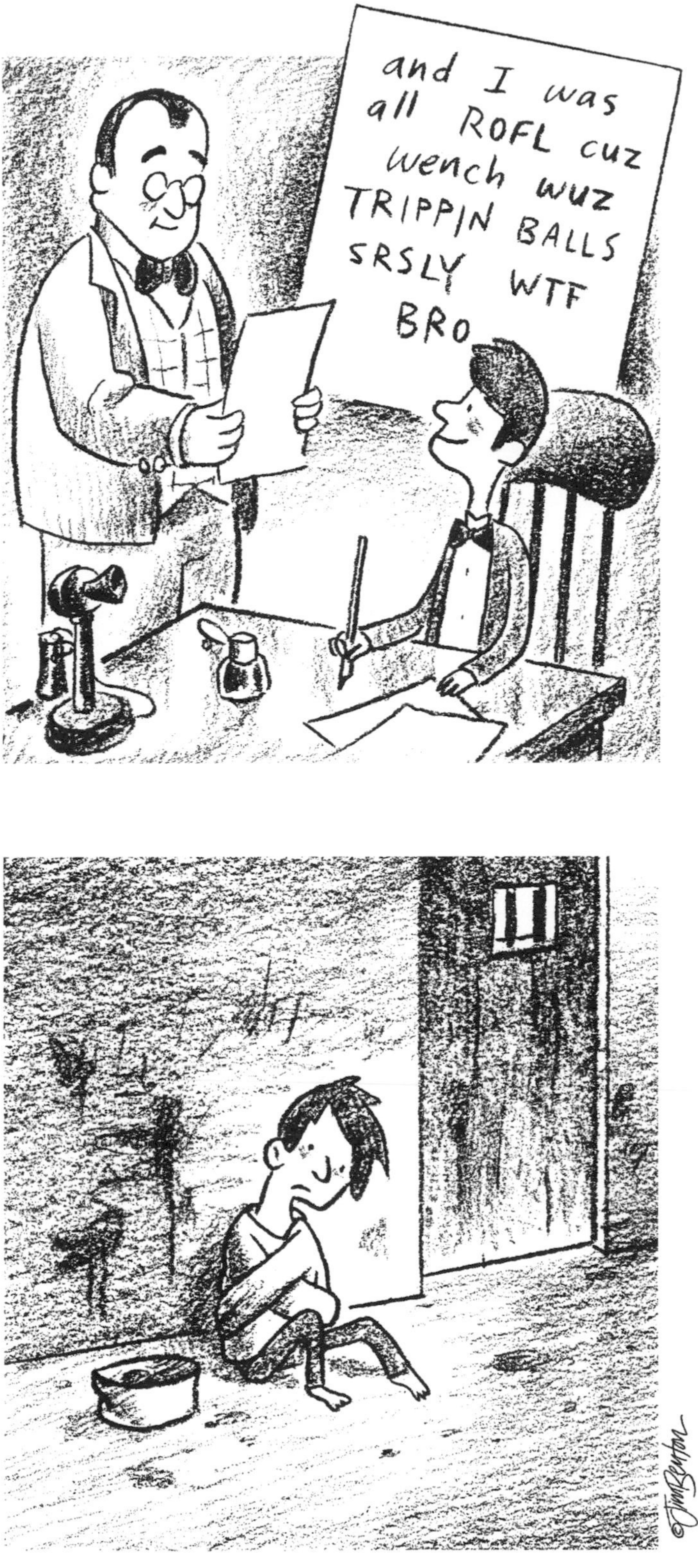
and I was all ROFL cuz wench wuz TRIPPIN BALLS SRSLY WTF BRO
©Jim Benton

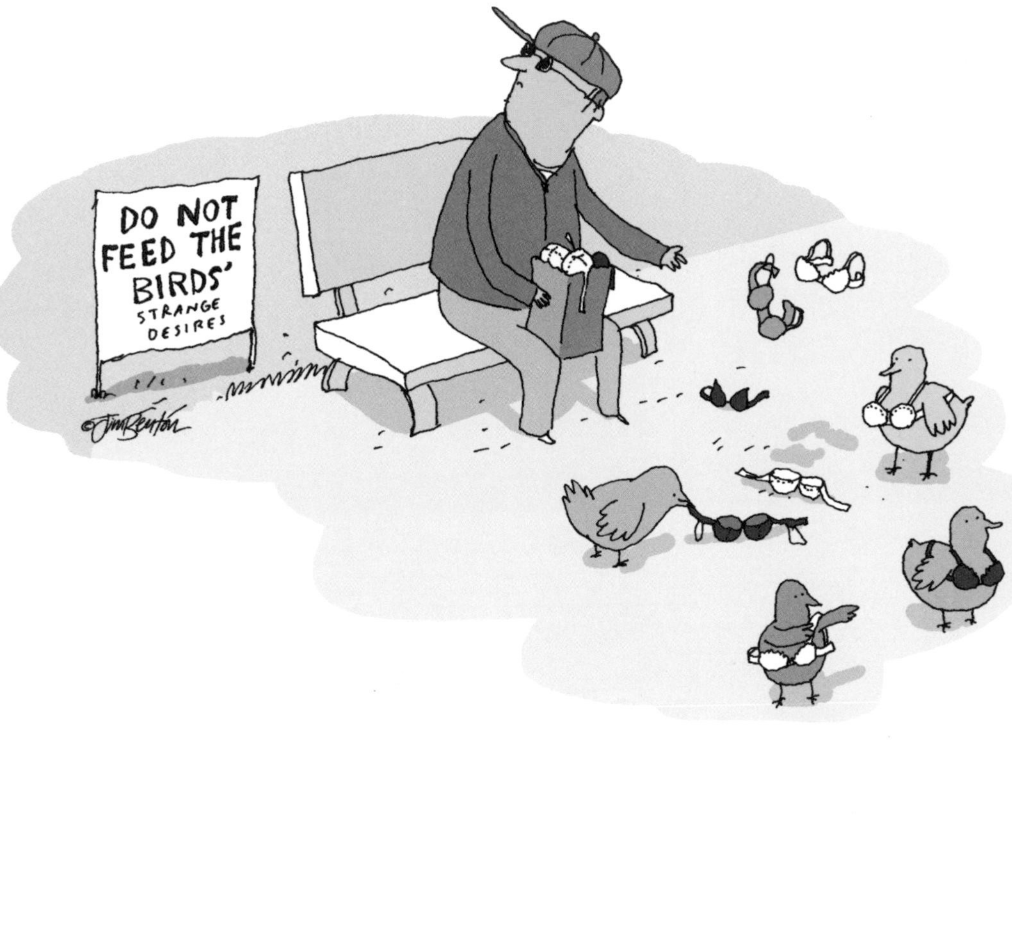
DO NOT FEED THE BIRDS' STRANGE DESIRES
©Jim Benton

Also available from NBM:

Kinky & Cosy

Nix

KINKY & COSY

Shocking! Disgusting! Meet the most dangerous twin girls in the universe! Their record of wrong doings, on purpose or not, will raise your hair on end. A darkly subversive collection of cynical comics gags that is sweeping Europe. Nothing is sacred for these two lil' monsters! South Park meets Monty Python.

8 1/2 x 6, 96pp., full color hardcover; $15.99,

ISBN 978-1-56163-604-4

A Home for Mr. Easter

Brooke A. Allen

A HOME FOR MR. EASTER
BROOKE A. ALLEN

You will love this crazy energetic book by a refreshing new talent! Tesana has never really fit into anything before but her daydreams. But when making an attempt to connect to her peers by joining in a pep rally planning committee she suddenly discovers a little white rabbit that lays brightly colored eggs. Realizing that she may have found the real life Easter bunny, Tesana embarks on an epic quest in an effort to get him back to his natural habitat and into safe hands. However as she progresses on her fanciful journey she gains more and more undesired attention until the quest becomes an increasingly madcap race to stay ahead of greedy pursuers and find a safe place for her new friend...wherever that place may be. It's Tesana against the world!

6x9, 208pp, B&W, trade pb, $13.99,

ISBN 978-1-56163-580-1

See more and order at nbmpub.com

We have over 200 titles,
See our complete list at nbmpub.com
NBM
160 Broadway, Suite 700, East Wing,
New York, NY 10038
Catalog available by request
If ordering by mail add $4 P&H 1st item,
$1 each addt'l

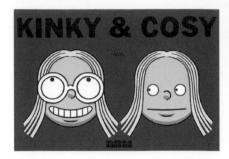

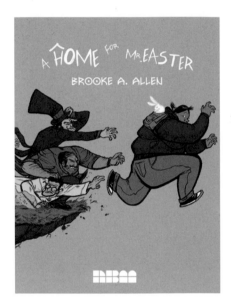